RIOJA AND ITS WINES

by

Ron Scarborough

SURVIVAL BOOKS • LONDON • ENGLAND

First published 2000

Survival Books Limited, Suite C, Third Floor
Standbrook House, 2-5 Old Bond Street
London W1X 3TB, United Kingdom
① (+44) 0207-493 4244, ✆ (+44) 0207-491 0605
✉ info@survivalbooks.net
🖳 survivalbooks.net

British Library Cataloguing in Publication Data.
A CIP record for this book is available from the British Library.
ISBN 1 901130 31 2

Printed and bound in Finland by WS Bookwell
Tenhusentie 3, FIN-51900 Juva, Finland

ACKNOWLEDGEMENTS

This book would not have been possible without the help and encouragement of many people, and I offer my sincere appreciation to each and everyone. The initial enthusiasm was sparked by Peter Read, followed immediately by a visit to Haro, where Alberto Hagemann and Susana Lacuesta offered further encouragement and invaluable help. The tourist office in Logroño, and in particular, Aurora Barcenilla, have generously provided a wealth of information, including the photographs used in this book. The *Consejo Regulador* have offered every assistance – particular thanks go to Berta Bartolomé González and Concha Peñaranda Díez, who provided invaluable information. Much gratitide to Carmen Merino Lozano, who (through a totally chance encounter) introduced my wife Patricia and I, in the most enthusiastic and entertaining way, to the history and culture of La Rioja. Many thanks also to Agustin Garcia at the Spanish Tourist Office in London and Javier Equerro at *Diario la Rioja* in Logroño, and also to Bernard Robin.

Much appreciation to everyone who provided information and took the time and trouble to read and comment on the draft versions, in particular, Karen and John Verheul and Peter Read. Not forgetting the hospitality of Barbara and John Webber in France, when we stayed en route on our numerous visits to the Rioja region. I would also like to thank Joanna Styles for her proof-reading and give a special thank you to Jim Watson (① UK 01708-813609) for the superb illustrations, maps and cover.

What Readers and Reviewers Have Said About Survival Books

When you buy a model plane for your child, a video recorder, or some new computer gizmo, you get with it a leaflet or booklet pleading 'Read Me First', or bearing large friendly letters or bold type saying 'IMPORTANT – follow the instructions carefully'. This book should be similarly supplied to all those entering France with anything more durable than a 5-day return ticket. – It is worth reading even if you are just visiting briefly, or if you have lived here for years and feel totally knowledgeable and secure. But if you need to find out how France works then it is indispensable. Native French people probably have a less thorough understanding of how their country functions. – Where it is most essential, the book is most up to the minute.

Living France

We would like to congratulate you on this work: it is really super! We hand it out to our expatriates and they read it with great interest and pleasure.

ICI (Switzerland) AG

Rarely has a 'survival guide' contained such useful advice – This book dispels doubts for first-time travelers, yet is also useful for seasoned globetrotters – In a word, if you are planning to move to the USA or go there for a long-term stay, then buy this book both for general reading and as a ready-reference.

American Citizens Abroad

It is everything you always wanted to ask but didn't for fear of the contemptuous put down – The best English-language guide – Its pages are stuffed with practical information on everyday subjects and are designed to complement the traditional guidebook.

Swiss News

Let's say it at once. David Hampshire's *Living and Working in France* is the best handbook ever produced for visitors and foreign residents in this country; indeed, my discussion with locals showed that it has much to teach even those born and bred in *l'Hexagone*. – It is Hampshire's meticulous detail which lifts his work way beyond the range of other books with similar titles. Often you think of a supplementary question and search for the answer in vain. With Hampshire this is rarely the case. – He writes with great clarity (and gives French equivalents of all key terms), a touch of humor and a ready eye for the odd (and often illuminating) fact. – This book is absolutely indispensable.

The Riviera Reporter

What Readers and Reviewers Have Said About Survival Books

What a great work, wealth of useful information, well-balanced wording and accuracy in details. My compliments!

Thomas Müller

This handbook has all the practical information one needs to set up home in the UK – The sheer volume of information is almost daunting – Highly recommended for anyone moving to the UK.

American Citizens Abroad

A very good book which has answered so many questions and even some I hadn't thought of – I would certainly recommend it.

Brian Fairman

A mine of information – I might have avoided some embarrassments and frights if I had read it prior to my first Swiss encounters – Deserves an honoured place on any newcomer's bookshelf.

English Teachers Association, Switzerland

Covers just about all the things you want to know on the subject – In answer to the desert island question about *the one* how-to book on France, this book would be it – Almost 500 pages of solid accurate reading – This book is about enjoyment as much as survival.

The Recorder

It is so funny – I love it and definitely need a copy of my own – Thanks very much for having written such a humorous and helpful book.

Heidi Guiliani

A must for all foreigners coming to Switzerland.

Antoinette O'Donoghue

A comprehensive guide to all things French, written in a highly readable and amusing style, for anyone planning to live, work or retire in France.

The Times

A concise, thorough account of the DOs and DON'Ts for a foreigner in Switzerland – Crammed with useful information and lightened with humourous quips which make the facts more readable.

American Citizens Abroad

Covers every conceivable question that might be asked concerning everyday life – I know of no other book that could take the place of this one.

France in Print

ABOUT THE AUTHOR

Born Ronald Frank Scarborough in Grimsby (Lincolnshire, England) in 1933 and educated at the local Wintringham Grammar School, the author qualified as a pharmacist from the Leicester School of Pharmacy in 1957. A keen sportsman he played football and cricket for his school, college and also local Grimsby and Leicester teams.

In 1964 he opened his own pharmacy in Bracknell, Berkshire and then six years later purchased a pharmacy and adjoining wine merchant's in historic Eton, near Windsor Castle, where he had the privilege of holding the Royal Appointment as Pharmacist to Her Majesty Queen Elizabeth II. It was here that his love of wine began, studying and tasting wines, and travelling widely in France and other European countries, including Spain.

In 1977, he bought his third pharmacy, moving with his wife and three children to Lowestoft in East Anglia to pursue his other great passion, sailing. He sold this pharmacy in 1992, becoming semi-retired and thus able to devote more time to travelling and furthering his enjoyment of wine. This led to a passion for Rioja and its wines, which culminated in the publication of this book.

> **"A woman drove me to drink, and I never even had the courtesy to thank her."**
> **W. C. Fields**

To Patricia with love

Grape Picking

CONTENTS

INTRODUCTION

This book has been written for both seasoned and potential wine lovers. It provides a wealth of information about Rioja and its wines, highlights their diversity and quality, acquaints you with this unspoiled wine region and smoothes your path to visiting Rioja's *bodegas* (wineries). Arriving for the first time in La Rioja, speaking little Spanish and certainly no Basque, I expected to find clearly signposted wine routes and ever-open *bodegas*. The reality was totally different. Thus ***Rioja and its Wines*** was conceived, a complete, pocket-sized guide containing every-thing you need to know about this fascinating and compact region in north-east Spain, and the wines produced there.

La Rioja (pronounced ree-ok-a) is often overlooked due to the sheer volume of wines now available world-wide, but has not been slow to evolve and make the most of its strengths. Forget any pre-conceived ideas you have about all Riojan wines being oak-aged – their young, un-oaked *jóvenes* (*sin crianza*) wines are fresh and fruity and far superior to wines from many other countries. The newer-style wines produced with less oak-ageing add another dimension of fruitiness, body and style to Riojan wines, while the aged *crianza*, *reserva* and *gran reserva* wines are wonderfully smooth and complex, and a match for any in the world – without the often ruinous prices! They also have the bonus of being ready for drinking when released for sale, without the need to be stored for years before they can be enjoyed.

To help you make the most out of a visit to Rioja, this book is divided into convenient sections. The chapter on the bodegas contains essential information for anyone planning to visit Rioja, including opening hours and the languages spoken, which will save you valuable time and allow you to concentrate on the *really important* job of tasting and buying wine.

Rioja and its Wines also contains historical information regarding the *bodegas* including when they were founded, the style of building, and details of the methods of wine production employed and the grape varieties used. The suggested wine routes will help you find the *bodegas* and visit places of interest along the way, and includes restaurants and hotels en route– all of which is designed to make your visit to Rioja as enjoyable and care-free as possible. For readers who are new to the world of wine, I have included a chapter on buying and storing wine, wine tasting, detecting faults, and wine and health.

Visiting Rioja, you will find wines rarely seen in other areas of Spain, let alone outside the country. When Rioja's wealth of superb wines is added to the region's fine cuisine, leisurely pace of life, beautiful unspoiled scenery, colourful history and architecture, and Rioja's friendly, fun-loving people (eagerly awaiting the next lively *fiesta*), you have the recipe for an enduring love affair. Once visited and beguiled by its magic, this fascinating region will draw you back time and time again. All its seasons have their particular allure, but my favourite is early November, when the mass of colourful vine leaves will take your breath away.

La Rioja is one of the world's best kept secrets and has been compared with Tuscany in the '60s and '70s before the hordes of tourists arrived – so visit this fascinating unspoiled region now – before someone else spoils it!

Salud!   **Ron Scarborough**
                                                   March 2000

"No verse can give pleasure for long, nor last, that is written by drinkers of water."
                                                   Horace

We're going to Rioja to taste its delicious wine,
And see the ancient buildings, they really are so fine,
I cannot wait to get to Haro and its exquisite little square,
With *tapas* and a glass of wine, there's really nothing to compare.

With so much to see in Logroño, wherever do we start?
Let's try *Calle Mayor* – that's in the oldest part.
We'll meet up with our Riojan friends, they really are such fun,
They love their food and wine and to frolic in the sun.

With pride they show you all around and take you to their heart,
Rioja's gems are everywhere, wherever will they start?
There are castles and picturesque villages, so much for us to see,
But there's one thing for certain – there'll be a winery!

I'd better watch those tastings, they always make me lurch,
I'll stagger in the village and miss another stunning church.
Rioja's not just oaked *crianza* wines, as distinctive as they are
There's lots of *jóvenes* – to beat them you'll have to travel far.

The newer *semi-crianzas* are a fruitier, less oaky style of wine
It is the French oak, not the Yankee, that makes them really fine,
And whisper 'CS' softly – Tempranillo's not the only grape,
But with tradition and innovation, Rioja's really in great shape.

Visit in the autumn, the colours will delight,
And your eyes will mist at the beauty of this truly wondrous sight.
Then take an uplifting journey on the ancient Pilgrims' Way
Joining many others with an urgent need to pray,
And feel so very thankful after all those travels long
You've found this enchanting land, where you feel that you belong.

Let's toast Rioja and its wines, so very justly praised,
And with our new found friends and all our glasses raised
We listen to the proverb that says that 'all is well'
When you see pink elephants in the *Calle Laurel*!

Ron Scarborough

Old Rioja

1.

HISTORY

L a Rioja has a history of vine cultivation stretching back over a thousand years, with records showing official recognition was given to Riojan wines as long ago as 1102. In the Middle Ages, Riojan wines were so important to the economy that in 1635 the Mayor of Logroño banned carriages from passing along the roads near to the bodegas, worried that they would disturb the wines. Rioja's commitment to quality dates back to 1650 when official documents make the first reference to quality control. The year 1787 saw the *Real Sociedad Económica de Cosecheros de Rioja* (Royal Economic Society of Rioja Wine Producers) established, with the aim, not only of encouraging the cultivation of vines and wine production, but also its commercial development.

Riojan wines are included in the oldest *denominación de origen* (equivalent to the French *appellation contrôlée*) in Spain and were officially recognised in 1926 with the establishment of the *Consejo Regulador* (regulatory board). From their headquarters in Logroño the *Consejo* designate the boundaries of the wine producing regions, the grape varieties which can be cultivated, the maximum yields permitted, the production and ageing process that can be used – and they also issue the 'labels of guarantee' found on every bottle. The board attained legal status in 1945 and finally became officially established in 1953. The *Reglamento de la Denominación de Origen y de su Consejo Regulador*, passed in 1970, established the guarantee of origin and gave the controlling authority a more clearly defined structure and responsibility for quality. In 1991, a Ministerial Order granted an additional and superior designation to be added to the wines of Rioja, making them the first, and to date, only, wines in Spain to attain the ranking of *Denominación de Origen Calificada Rioja (DOCa)*.

A number of commemorative events to mark the 75th anniversary of the *Consejo Regulador* are being held throughout the year 2000.

Rioja's connection with France began in the second half of the 19th century when French vineyards were affected first with mildew and then with phylloxera, the parasite that was to destroy practically all French vines. Inevitably, some of the Bordeaux wine producers came to the Rioja region and soon realised that, although conditions were different from those they knew in Bordeaux, it would still be possible to produce good wines – as was subsequently shown when they vastly improved wine production in the region. Haro, due to its good rail links from France and other regions of Spain, tends to be the location of the oldest bodegas, while Logroño (in the centre of the region) is the natural administrative centre.

The name 'Rioja' is derived from '*Río*' (river in Spanish) and '*Oja*' which is the River Oja, a stream rather than a river. It is one of life's oddities that the larger Rivers Ebro or Tirón were not used when naming the region – perhaps 'Rioebro' or 'Riotirón' would not have *quite* the same ring – but the wine would still taste as good!

Rioja can also lay claim to the origins of the Castilian (Spanish) language. The 13th century poet, Gonzalo de Berceo, was the first person to write in Castilian rather than Latin, immortalising the wines of Rioja in verse. Today, from these humble origins in Rioja, some 300 million people speak Castilian world-wide.

Production

The La Rioja region encircles the River Ebro in north-east Spain and is ideal for growing vines. There are some 50,000 hectares (123,548 acres) under cultivation, yielding an average of 190 million litres of wine annually, 75 per cent red (*tinto*) with the remainder white (*blanco*) and rosé (*rosado*). The Rioja wine region is subdivided into three districts or sub-regions (as shown on the map inside the back cover): the *Rioja Alta* west of Logroño, the *Rioja Alavesa* that forms part of the province of Alava in the Basque Country (*País Vasco, Euskadi*) and the *Rioja Baja* south-east of Logroño, parts of which are situated in the neighbouring region of Navarra.

This seemingly haphazard arrangement owes more to the political structure of post-democratic Spain than to the actual distribution of the vineyards, although the soil and climate peculiarities also influence the classification of the three wine-producing sub-regions and affect the taste of the wines. Rioja Alta and Rioja Alavesa are 400 to 500 metres above sea level and therefore have a slightly cooler climate than the Rioja Baja, which helps produce wines of the highest quality.

La Rioja Alavesa, the smallest of the three sub-regions, is situated north of the River Ebro near the area known as Conchas de Haro, a little to the east of Logroño. The combination of soil (mostly calcareous clay), the high proportion of Tempranillo grapes used, the temperate climate and the south-facing vineyards ensure that the Rioja Alavesa produces some of the best wines, if not the best, in the region. Although some of the wines are light, in general they are elegant, soft and fruity with the distinctive bouquet of the Tempranillo grape. They mature more rapidly than those from the Rioja Alta, but tend not to be so long-lived. Much smaller amounts of white wine, with a good acid balance, are made from the Viura and Malvasía grapes.

La Rioja Alta lies entirely within the region of Rioja extending south of the River Ebro from the Conchas de Haro in the west to just beyond Logroño in the east (there is also a small northern area around Abalos). Due to the microclimate (every country and wine-producing region claims a micro-climate), coupled with the mixture of calcareous clay, alluvial silt and ferruginous clay, oenologists have subdivided the area from west to east into the zones of Cuzcurrita, Haro, San Asensio and Cenicero-Fuenmayor. The more hilly and wetter western area produces wines which are more acidic and lower in alcohol than those from Cenicero, where there is a transition in climate from humid to semi-arid and more calcareous soils suiting the Tempranillo grape better.

The Rioja Alta traditionally uses a higher percentage of Mazuelo, Graciano and Garnacha grapes in its red wines along with the basic Tempranillo, and its wines tend to have a fresher bouquet and be a little more acidic and longer lasting than Alavesa reds. The whites are made from Viura and Malvasía, plus some Garnacha Blanca, but as some large bodegas use a blend of wine from grapes grown in Alta and Alavesa, it can be difficult to be specific. This variation in grapes, areas, vinification, etc., is one of the reasons many people (your author included) find the area and its wines so appealing. The wines produced are long-lived and medium-bodied, with a huge capacity for ageing.

La Rioja Baja is the sub-region east of Logroño along the River Ebro to Alfaro in the south-east, with a large part in the area of Rioja south of the river. There is also a small strip situated within the region of Navarra to the north. The soils are mostly alluvial silt and ferruginous clay, and the climate is semi-arid Mediterranean. The main grape used is the red Garnacha tinta, which produces wines that are high in alcohol, powerful and full-bodied, but quick to oxidise and not as fine as the other two areas. The wines are often used for blending, although naturally there are exceptions. However, *Bodegas Berberana* (now *Arco Bodegas Unidas*) have successfully experimented with the planting of Tempranillo and Viura in the calcareous soils found in the higher part of the area at Monte Yerga.

Climate: The La Rioja region slopes from west to east with the climate becoming increasingly drier and hotter in the east owing to the Mediterranean influence. The Rioja Alta in the west has an Atlantic climate, the Rioja Alavesa a mixture of Atlantic and Mediterranean, while the Rioja Baja has a hotter Mediterranean climate. This hotter climate results in riper, more alcoholic and generally less subtle wines (again with exceptions), which also mature more quickly and are generally cheaper. The La Rioja region can be very cold in winter, which coupled with short hot summers, forces the roots of the vines to fight hard for nourishment, resulting in grapes with an abundance of flavour. The winemakers (*bodegueros*) skilfully blend these grapes from one, two or even all three of Rioja's sub-regions to produce their wines.

Soil: There are three main types of soil in La Rioja. Clay-limestone soil is found on terraced slopes and small plots of land in Rioja Alavesa and Rioja Alta, and produces wines with a good colour. Ferrous-clay, which is found on sloping land throughout Rioja, is hard and a reddish-brown colour, and is good for producing rosés and light reds with medium body. Finally there is alluvial soil, a mixture of fine mud, silt and sand deposited in the ice age, and found near rivers throughout the three sub-regions, which helps produce medium-bodied whites and reds.

> **At the next wine tasting, why not try "a strong taste of alluvial, with a hint of silt and sand - probably from the Ice Age".**

Topography: Rioja's northern border is marked by the Sierra de Cantabria mountain range, which forms a natural protection for the vines against the cooler winds and rain from the Atlantic. To the south lie the Sierra de la Demanda and Las Cameros mountain ranges. The River Ebro, running through the region, has a host of vineyards on both banks, and helps provide irrigation for the vines.

Pruning: Pruning in Rioja typically consists of shaping the vine into three arms, each of which has two shoots, called *en vaso* ('glass' in Spanish), because the pruned vines resemble a wine glass. Each shoot has two visible buds from which the new shoots form the following year. The *en vaso* method minimises maintenance work and protects the vines from strong winds and excessive sunshine, although it also makes mechanical harvesting impossible. The vines for the newer style wines are trailed along wires called *en espaldera* (cordon trellising), exposing grapes more to the sun and permitting them to be harvested mechanically.

Harvesting: This is traditionally carried out by hand using curved knives (*corquetes*) and is usually done in October (but sometimes begins in the last week of September) starting in the Rioja Baja and finishing in the Rioja Alta. As the harvest can take 30 to 40 days, this effectively means that it can continue into November, although it is usually completed in October. The grapes are collected in wicker baskets with a capacity of 15 to 20kg (33 to 44lb) and deposited in wooden crates (*comportas*) containing 80 to 120kg (176 to 265lb). These are then emptied into tractor-trailers for transportation to the bodega to commence the different winemaking processes.

For white (*blanco*) wine the whole grape goes into the dejuicers where the stems and skins are removed leaving the must (juice), which is transferred to the fermentation tanks. The technique of slow fermentation at low temperatures gives the white wines a fresher and fruitier taste, and this method is now being used to make rosé wines.

With rosé (*rosado*) wine the grapes are de-stemmed and lightly crushed before being transferred to the dejuicing tanks, where the maceration of the liquid, along with the skin, is carefully controlled. Once the must is obtained, the suspended material is decanted for a day and this almost clear liquid passes to the fermentation tanks.

To produce red (*tinto*) wines, there are two distinct processes. Nowadays, the most common method consists of removing the skin in the de-stemmer/crusher before fermentation, producing wines suitable for long ageing. During carbonic maceration, the second process, the whole grape with its skin passes to the fermentation tanks, producing smooth wines with good body and dark colour, suitable for drinking in their first year. In both cases, fermentation at a constant temperature ensures that none of the aroma of the must is lost. When fermentation is complete the emptying process takes place, the solid residues are removed and the wine is transferred to storage tanks and subjected to quality checks.

The *Consejo Regulador* (the Regulatory Board of the *Denominación de Origen Calificada Rioja*) has very strict controls with high standards, and only after carrying out quality control tests with sensory and chemical testing do they decide whether the wine warrants the *Denominación de Origen Calificada Rioja* classification. Tests are performed in the laboratories of the *Consejo Regulador* in Logroño and the *Estación de Viticultura y Enología de Haro,* followed by analytical checks at the *Casa del Viño* in Laguardia, in the *Estacións Enológica* in Olite (Navarra) or Haro. The latter laboratory has been in operation since 1892, while the one in Laguardia since 1982 only. The *Consejo Regulador* in Logroño has impressive premises with a dedicated team of specialists manning its technical, legal, administrative and promotional services. All wines for export must be approved in Haro by a committee of between five and seven members, with the final export permission decided by a majority vote.

Yields: The maximum yield permitted, in accordance with the protection of the quality of the wine, is 6,500kg (14,329lb) per hectare for red grapes and 9,000kg (19,841lb) per hectare for white, although the overall yield for the whole denomination is usually lower. The annual average production of Rioja is around 200 million litres, 75 per cent of which are red wines, with the remainder rosés and whites.

Ageing: The ageing process gives Riojan wines their special character, with no other wine region in the world maturing such large quantities of wine in oak barrels (*barricas*). The construction and capacity of the 225-litre capacity Bordeaux casks (*barrique bordelaise*) is regulated by law. After one to three years spent in the oak casks, with regular racking to remove the lees (sediment), the wine then spends six months to six years in the bottle before being released onto the market. At this stage Rioja wines can *be drunk and enjoyed immediately,* although *reservas* and *gran reservas* (see below) will continue to improve in the bottle for many years, producing complex, velvety delights.

Classification and Labelling: Riojan wines are classified into one of four categories, depending on the length of maturation in barrel and bottle undergone before being released for sale. At the bottom of the scale are the *Joven* or *Sin Crianza* (young wines) in their first or second year, whose wines have a greenish-coloured label and show the year e.g. *Cosecha 1999.* They are young red, white or rosé wines, fresh and fruity made without oak ageing, which are refreshing when drunk chilled. They comprise up to 60 per cent of Rioja's total production and are mainly sold in Spain, although their export is increasing. A small percentage of *sin-crianza* wines are also aged for a few months in oak, although the regulations do not allow this to be stated on the label. Also with a greenish label are the *Conjunto Varias Cosechas (CVC)* wines, which are a blend of various vintages comprising 15 per cent of the region's total wine production.

Crianza wines have a brighter red label and are in their third year of ageing when released, the reds having at least one year in oak, the whites or rosés at least six months, with the remainder of the ageing process spent in bottle. *Crianza* wines are more complex than *sin crianza* as better quality base wine is used and they have also had the benefit of ageing in oak casks. Many wine drinkers consider that *crianza* wines produce the best balance between an oaky taste and good fruit flavour, even preferring them to *reservas* or *gran reservas*. Although ideal for drinking and enjoying on their own, they are robust enough to accompany *chorizo*, peppers, *jamón ibérico* and any main course.

Reserva wines have a brown-red label. In years with a good vintage, the best wines have the potential to be made into *reservas*, when the reds are aged for a minimum of three years, and rosés and whites for two years. Red *reservas* spend at least one year in oak casks, and rosés and whites a minimum of six months. With just 10 per cent of Riojan wines classified as *reservas*, they are obviously rarer and more expensive than *crianzas*. Some bodegas also make wines designated as *Reserva Especial*, which is an unofficial name for a special wine made only in exceptional years (somewhere in quality between a *reserva* and a *gran reserva*).

Gran Reserva wines have a darker brown-red label and have either been chosen from an exceptional vintage or from a blend of *reservas* deemed capable of further oak ageing. The minimum ageing is five years, with a minimum of two years in oak, although some bodegas give them at least an additional year before bottling them, plus several years in bottle. *Gran reserva* whites and rosés spend a minimum of six months in oak, followed by bottle ageing, but are extremely rare. The *gran reserva* category is the highest level of quality and accounts for only a small percentage of Riojan wine production.

> **"No man having drunk old wine straitway desireth new; for he saith, the old is better."**
> **St Luke, Chapter 5, Verse 39**

The '80s were marked by some significant and far-reaching changes in Rioja. Over-production, plummeting prices and falling demand prompted some forward-thinking Riojan producers into action to combat the threat from the new world wine revolution of fruity, full-flavoured wines. The problem of adjusting to this competition without alienating traditional producers and buyers was resolved by a willingness to experiment with controversial techniques, which are now more widely accepted. These new winemaking techniques produced fruitier, balanced, elegant wines with spicier oaky tastes, using a combination of longer maceration of the grape skins during fermentation, modern temperature-controlled stainless steel equipment and ageing facilities.

Occasionally there was also a change from American oak to the less tightly grained French oak, and more frequent renewal of barrels. New vineyard management techniques were introduced, with quality and yields kept under stricter control. The vines were trained along wires (*en espaldera*), instead of the traditional Rioja *en vaso* bush method, resulting in increased sunlight and ventilation, and allowing work around the vines by mechanical means. This also ensured consistent ripening and to limit the yield, a new strict 'timed-pruning' method was introduced and the grapes were harvested at the optimum time. Quality selection of grapes is still a critical factor and even the hoary old chestnut of irrigation reared its ugly head – excess irrigation results in over-production and too little can be disastrous – winemaking is never easy!

The end result has been that Rioja now has an even wider armoury of styles to compete on the increasingly competitive world market, helping to remind wine drinkers not to overlook the wonderful selection of excellent wines available from this small, quality-conscious and progressive wine area of Spain.

> **"Quickly, bring me a beaker of wine, so that I may wet my mind and say something clever."**
> **Aristophanes: Knights**

Grape Varieties

The *Consejo Regulador* approves seven varieties of grapes, four red and three white, with a special dispensation for the use of Cabernet Sauvignon on an experimental basis. *Tempranillo*, the backbone of red Riojan wines, is a thick-skinned, very black glossy grape. It produces smooth and fruity-flavoured wines with a ruby red colour, 10.5 to 13 per cent alcohol, and a strawberry and vanilla taste intensified by oak ageing. The low level of oxidase enzymes makes it suitable, not only for ageing, but also for young wines.

The name Tempranillo comes from *temprano* meaning 'early', with ripening mid to late September, although in practice grapes are picked around the 10th of October. Tempranillo, which has good acid balance and a characteristic bouquet, is known in the La Mancha and Valdepeñas regions as *cencibel*, and growers claim that wine made from the Riojan Tempranillo and *cencibel* grown *in the same vineyard*, produce wine with a different taste. Tempranillo is also known as *ull de llebre* in Catalonia, *ojo de liebre* in Penedès, as *tinto fino* – the fine dark one – in Ribera del Duero, *tinto de toro* and *tinto del país* in Castile-Leon, and *aragonez* and *tinta roriz* in Portugal. Tempranillo in some quarters is also claimed to be related to *pinot noir* (a grape prone to mutation) and it has also been suggested that it could be the *valdepeñas* grape grown in the central valley of California. The latest DNA testing techniques will no doubt reveal all, removing another of life's mysteries . .

The *Mazuelo* (red) grape, known in other parts of Spain as *carineña* and in southern France as *carignan*, is also low in oxidase enzymes with a stable colour, making it the perfect complement for Tempranillo in wines to be aged. Its bouquet suggests ripe fruit and it produces wines with a lot of tannin and high acidity. In hot years this tough little grape can achieve 13.5 degrees of alcohol, imparting longevity to Riojan wines even when added in small amounts.

Garnacha Tinta (red) is a dark skinned grape, sometimes described as having a peppery taste. It is an ideal variety for producing rosé wines, but on its own it oxidises easily and is mainly used to strengthen reds with body and alcohol. However, at least one Riojan Bodega (*Martínez Bujanda*) produces a *varietal* (single grape) wine made entirely from Garnacha. It can produce wines of 16 degrees of alcohol in the Rioja Baja and is a vigorous grape, resistant to the mould oidium, but rather prone to mildew. Garnacha is also known as *lladoner*, *grenache* in the Rhône in France and as *aragon* in Castile-Leon.

Graciano (red) is a small, black, thick-skinned grape which fell out of favour some years ago, but is now back with Rioja's promotion to DOCa status. Excellent single grape Graciano wines are produced in Rioja, first by *Viña Ijalba* and also by *Bodegas de la MarquesA, SMS*. It is no surprise that these two high quality bodegas have used their dedication and considerable expertise with this difficult but high quality, perfumed grape to produce interesting 100 per cent Graciano wines. The grape itself is acidic and although its wines are tannic when young, they mature well and elegantly under the *crianza* system. In the Languedoc in France, Graciano is known as *morrastel* – not the Monastrell grown widely in south-east Spain – and it is believed that it could also possibly be the *xeres* grape grown in California.

The *Viura* or Macabeo (white) grape contains high acidity, which makes it ideal not only for young white wines, but also for wines to be aged. It also complements the grape varieties used in red wines. Traditionally it used to be added in small quantities to give a certain fire and brilliance to the reds, but this practice is dying out, although it is still added to some Rioja Alavesa wines to improve the acid balance. With the newer, cold-fermented, *joven* white wines, it has had a new lease of life, although sales of white Riojas are still well below those of reds. Viura is also called *Macabeo* in north and western Spain, and *Macabeu* in France. In the hands of skilled winemakers it can produce good aromatic, spicy-nosed wines, and although it is often picked early to retain acidity, it really needs to be fully ripe to develop its typical floral character. Viura is also the main grape for Cava, the Spanish sparkling wine made by the traditional method of fermentation in the bottle.

Malvasía (white) has its roots (not literally) in ancient Greece, its name being derived from the Greek port of Monemvasia, which was used in the middle ages to transport dessert wines to Europe. In Rioja, Malvasía is used together with Viura in oak-aged whites due to its good bouquet, balanced acidity and spiciness, and it also to help in the ageing process. Although rare nowadays, it used to be added to the blend when making red Riojan wines, and its reddish tinge when ripe has given it the name of *früher roter Malvasia* in Germany (*früher roter* is 'early red' in German). In Penedès it is called *subirat parent,* in Madeira it is *malmsey,* and in Italy and Crete a number of Malvasía varieties are grown.

Garnacha Blanca (white) is the white sibling of the red Garnacha grape, producing light wines lacking in acidity and having a dry aftertaste, which are ideal for early drinking. It is also used to help smooth out blends in under-ripe years. Garnacha Blanca is known as *Grenache Blanc* in France.

Cabernet Sauvignon, although not an official grape variety of Rioja, is also found in some red Riojas and has lots of character and blends well with Tempranillo. It needs ageing to make its best wine and has a characteristic blackcurrant bouquet and, when matured in new oak, a cedar-like aroma. It is being increasingly used in some bodegas for newer-style wines, although its use is vehemently opposed by some traditionalists.

Grape Blending: *Varietal* (single grape wines) Riojas of Tempranillo (or Garnacha, Graciano or even Mazuelo) are increasingly being made, although most producers still prefer to use their own individual combination of grapes for what they consider the perfect Riojan wine. The blend can even differ within the same bodega for wines earmarked for *crianza, reserva* and *gran reserva* development. Most blends use at least three of the major grapes and in the Rioja Alta it is quite common for producers to use all four. Bear in mind that not only the ripeness of individual grapes, but also the quality of the harvest determines a winemaker's choice of grapes and the quantities of each variety used, **therefore the grape proportions given in Chapter 2 (Rioja's Bodegas) may vary.**

Examples of the variations in grape varieties used in red *crianza* wines from various bodegas are shown below:

Rioja Alavesa:

- *Martínez Bujanda Valdemar* 1985 – 85 per cent Tempranillo, 15 per cent Mazuelo.

- *Marqúes de Riscal* 1985 – 90 per cent Tempranillo, 5 per cent Mazuelo, 5 per cent Graciano.

Rioja Baja:

- *Ondarre* 1986 – 60 per cent Tempranillo, 30 per cent Garnacha, 10 per cent Mazuelo.

- *Ontanon Artesa* 1988 – 60 per cent Tempranillo, 40 per cent Garnacha.

Rioja Alta:

- *CVNE* (pronounced 'Coonay') 1985 – 70 per cent Tempranillo, 15 per cent Garnacha, 10 per cent Mazuelo and 5 per cent Viura.

- *Marqués de Cáceres* 1985 – 100 per cent Tempranillo.

Some growers only use grapes from their own vineyards and their wines are known as 'single estate Riojas', although many buy in grapes as well as grow their own. Some even buy promising young wines and blend their own *cuvées* in their 'house style' (a consistent, recognisable style of their own) and put them through their own ageing process. However, most of the non-estate houses buy and blend grapes, not just from different grape growers, but from different sub-regions of Rioja. A small proportion of grapes from the Rioja Baja region are used by some winemakers in Rioja Alta and Rioja Alavesa to add ripeness, colour and strength to their wines. However, if the producer's label states a particular area, all the grapes used to make the wine must come from that area.

Oak

Ageing in oak barrels has always been part of the winemaking culture in Rioja – not for them the current fad of adding toasted oak chippings in a tea-bag to improve profits and hopefully the taste! The Rioja region is the wine world's largest user of oak, mainly American but also more expensive French oak. Traditional American oak has a more powerful flavour than

French and has a distinctive, slightly sweetish vanilla influence on wines. French oak, however, gives a more subtle flavour and fruitiness, being less dense, and the barrels are also made with thinner staves that allow for quicker development. In recent years, the practice of renewing barrels more often has led to the production of fruitier styles.

Long ageing in barrels develops a soft, mellow taste, which is reminiscent of cedar, or perhaps more surprisingly, a not unpleasant tobacco flavour, with the charring of the inside of barrels adding a toasty, slightly spicy aftertaste to the wine. In wine language, the term 'oaky' describes any or all of the above tastes.

If you are not a fan of the traditional oaked Riojan wines, newer-style wines are increasingly available. *Bodegas Palacio*, *Roda* and *Remelluri* use French oak almost exclusively, while others, such as *Bodega La Rioja Alta*, prefer American oak barrels and are returning to them. On the other hand, *Muga, Olarra* and *Lan*, for example, use one or both types of oak, depending on the style required. The new young, *joven (sin crianza)* un-oaked Riojas are another aspect of winemaking in the region and often have more taste and fruit than similar style wines from other regions of the world.

Oak gives wine flavour, colour and tannins, and also allows more contact with air than stainless steel, fibreglass or lined cement. For reasons not fully understood, there is a complex interaction between wine and oak barrels, but we do know that wine put into new barrels will obviously leech out more flavours. Nothing earth-shattering about that, but the clearing and stabilising effect, the varying flavours and the resulting smoothness produced are not so easily explained, and wine certainly ages more quickly in a barrel than a bottle due to the greater contact with air.

> "Wine comes in at the mouth and love comes in at the eye, that's all we shall know for truth before we grow old and die."
>
> **W. B. Yeats (a drinking song)**

> It is worth emphasising that although Riojan wines age and improve in the bottle, they have the advantage that they can be drunk and enjoyed immediately after they are released for sale. Compare this, for example, with classical Bordeaux reds, which although superb, need years of ageing to come to full maturity, which coupled with their original cost, ensures a high price and a long wait.

The 225-litre oak barrels (*barricas*), the size governed by law, are the optimum size for ageing. Larger barrels would not allow sufficient contact of wood with wine, while smaller ones would provide too much contact. The production of oak barrels is big business in the USA, where bourbon (whisky distilled from maize and rye) is required by law to be matured in *new* American oak barrels. This led to a continuous supply of old bourbon oak barrels, which have been the traditional means of ageing Riojan wines, and the Tempranillo grape's resistance to oxidation has ensured that wood ageing of Riojas has always been done on a large scale. American oak is a dense wood lacking in porosity and the barrel staves are cut thicker than in French barrels, ensuring that the wine matures more slowly due to the resulting reduced contact with oxygen.

However, the wider use of French oak and less time spent in barrels (which are also renewed more frequently), although producing more fruitiness and flavour, presents a problem for the *Consejo Regulador*. The current *crianza* categories signify ageing as a measure of quality and do not allow for these modern styles, and this problem will undoubtedly need to be addressed. For example, so called *semi-crianza* wines such as *Marqués de Griñon* or *Cosme Palacio*, which are only lightly oaked to maximise fruitiness, cannot be classified as *crianza*, not having spent the required 12 months in oak.

Increasingly, even the most traditional bodegas are modernising and using temperature controlled stainless steel tanks for the fermentation process. Even the staunchly traditional *R. López de Heredia,* founded in 1877, has called in the Australian viticultural flying doctor Richard Smart to advise – can the dreaded plastic cork be far away!

Los Barricas

2.

RIOJA'S BODEGAS

One of the joys of Riojan wines is the wonderful diversity of both the old and new styles produced by both large and small bodegas, but it can be frustrating after enjoying a bottle of wine not to be able to discover more about it. This chapter is designed to provide you with this much-needed information. It includes an alphabetical list of selected bodegas, historical and architectural information, wine names used on their labels, grape varieties, visiting hours for individuals and groups, and the languages spoken other than Spanish. The reference to a shop usually means that a bodega sells wines to the public – do not expect a supermarket! Some UK tour operators offer package holidays that include trips to bodegas where you can dine, taste and buy wines directly (see **Appendix H**).

Note that in most cases you must telephone and make an appointment beforehand – as far in advance as possible – telephone (℗) and fax (🖷) numbers are provided. Remember to pre-fix the number shown with the international code, e.g. 00 or 010, followed by Spain's country code (34) when calling from outside Spain. Note also that some Bodegas prefer weekday visits rather than at weekends.

The comparatively small region of Rioja contains around 380 bodegas and those listed in the following pages (around half the total number) have been included as they welcome visitors and offer tastings. It is not intended as a list of the best Riojan bodegas, although many of the best producers are included. Winegrowers are enthusiasts, producing wines with love and care often under difficult conditions, and welcome sharing their passion with visitors, obviously hoping that you will buy at least a few bottles. Bear in mind, to wine producers their wines are like beloved children and should not be treated lightly!

A *bodega* is the Spanish equivalent of an American winery or a French *château*, although the name (confusingly) is also used for a wine shop. *Provir* after a bodega's name, denotes that they belong to a group of 15 small to medium size, quality conscious bodegas who are eager to show you around. The names of the wines used on each bodega's labels are included in this chapter, although some simply use the name of the bodega itself, e.g. *Viña Amézola* and *Señorío Amézola* from *Bodegas Amézola de la Mora*.

Abeica Bodegas, *Provir* (Abalos, Alta ☏ 941 334 104, ✉ 941 308 009) was founded in 1988 and is a small family, medal-winning bodega with 30ha (74 acres) of vineyards and 250 barrels, as well as stainless steel fermentation tanks. Carbonic maceration is used for the *joven* wine labelled *Chulato*, which contains 90 per cent Tempranillo and 10 per cent Viura. The 100 per cent Tempranillo *Longrande crianzas* and *reservas* are excellent and full-flavoured (the 1996 *crianza* won a silver medal in France in 1999). Daily visits are by appointment and tours of the interesting religious and lay art in the village can also be organised on request.

Provir (*Productores Vitivinícolas Riojanos*) **is an organisation of small and medium-size bodegas, all family enterprises with a personal interest in welcoming visitors and upholding the best traditions of Riojan winemaking. There are around 15 members, indicated by Provir after the bodega's name.**

Afersa Bodegas (San Asensio, Alta, ☏ 941 457 394, ✉ 941 457 394) was founded in 1989 and is located in a picturesque setting with views of the River Ebro valley and Sierra de Cantabria mountains. The bodega has 5ha (12 acres) of vineyards and 150 barrels. Its *joven*, *crianza* and *reserva* wines are sold under the *Cerrillo Verballe* label. The *crianza* is made from Tempranillo, Garnacha and Mazuelo grapes, while the *reserva* also contains Graciano and the *joven* includes Viura. The *El Agozal* label is used for *joven* red, white and rosé wines. Visits are by appointment on weekday mornings and afternoons.

AGE Bodegas SA (Fuenmayor, Alta, ☏ 941 293 500, ✉ 941 293 501) was founded in 1881. The bodega has several old buildings dating from 1881 to 1913, with new buildings added in 1988 including a new vinification centre. In 1987, Guinness acquired a major share holding and invested millions of pounds turning it into one of Spain's most modern production facilities with some 3,000 barrels. Guinness sold out in the early '90s and AGE is now owned by **Bodegas y Bebidas**, with around 60 per cent of wines sold under the **Siglo** label. The bodega's own 50ha (123 acres) of vineyards supply just a small percentage of the grapes necessary, the bulk being bought-in locally.

The best known wine is the modern style, **Siglo Saco**, sold in bottles wrapped in jute sacking, which is marketed with various coloured labels, the black being the *gran reserva*. **Romeral** is used for the *sin crianza joven* red, white and rosé. The **Marqués del Pomeral** *gran reserva*, made in traditional style has more personality than the Siglo Saco and is of better quality. AGE's other brands include **Bodegas Las Veras, Viña Tere, Agessimo, Azpilcueta Martínez, Don Ernesto** and **Credencial. Bodegas y Bebidas** also own **Bodegas Campo Viejo** and **Bodegas Marqués del Puerto**. Group and individual visits are daily (except Sundays) by appointment, mornings and afternoons. There is a shop and English and French are spoken.

Aguirre Viteri, J. Higinio (Lapuebla de Labarca, Alavesa, ① 941 607 148) was founded in 1980 and has 10ha (25 acres) of vineyards. The original bodega has stone arches and underground cellars containing 5,500 litre wooden vats (over 150 years old), while a new bodega built in 1992 is ultra modern. Individual and group visits are by appointment mornings and afternoons, except Sunday, when they are mornings only.

Alavesas, Bodegas (Laguardia, Alavesa, ① 941 600 100, ⊑ 941 600 031). In 1972, Miguel Angel Alonso Samaniego put up the capital and a group of winegrowers provided the land to start this bodega, which has 5,500 barrels and 95ha (234 acres) of vineyards. Their most important brand is **Solar de Salmaniego**, which includes *reservas* and *gran reservas* of quality and elegance made with 100 per cent Tempranillo. Other brand names are **Bodegas Alavesas Viño Joven, Castillo de Bodala, Solar de Iriarte** and **Señorío de Berbete**, which are used mainly for *joven* wines and red *crianzas*. Visits by individuals and groups are by appointment, mornings and afternoons, and there is a shop.

Alberto Guitiérrez Andrés, Bodegas (Haro, Alta ① 941 310 023, ⊑ 941 310 393). Individual visits are by appointment, Tuesdays to Fridays, 11am to 1pm and 4 to 5pm, except for the first two weeks in July and last two weeks of October.

Alejos Bodegas (Agoncillo, Baja ☎ 941 437 051, 🖷 941 437 077) is a modern designed and equipped bodega founded in 1976 with 11ha (27 acres) of vineyards and 500 barrels. The *Alabanza* label is used for a *crianza* and **Duque de Frías** for *joven* red, white and rosé. Visits by individuals or groups are by appointment. English, French and German are spoken.

Amézola de la Mora, Bodegas (Torremontalvo, Alta, ☎ 941 454 532, 🖷 941 454 537) was restarted by a lawyer, Inigo Amezola de la Mora, in a historic castle situated between Logroño and Haro, where the 130-year old cellars were totally re-equipped in 1986. The bodega's buildings are in the middle of 100ha (247 acres) of vineyards and the bodega has 2,000 barrels, a third being French oak. The estate grown, quality, medium bodied red wines, **Viña Amézola** *crianza* and **Señorío Amézola** *reserva*, are excellent and full of flavour (both are made with 90 per cent Tempranillo and 10 per cent Mazuelo). Individual and group visits are by appointment, mornings and afternoons (French is spoken).

Antigua Usanza, *Provir* (San Vicente de la Sonsierra, Alta ☎ 941 334 156, 🖷 941 334 156). In 1989, the distillery **Licorera Albendense** founded its own bodega, equipping it with stainless steel tanks and 500 barrels, half in French oak. They buy wines from Rioja Alavesa. The fruity young *joven* and *crianza* are labelled **Viña Azai** and sold only in Spain, while the **Antigua Usanza** *joven* and *crianza*, soft and supple with a little fruit, are also sold abroad (e.g. in the UK). The subsidiary label is **Peña Bajenza**. Individual visits are by appointment.

> **"Wine brings to life the hidden secrets of the soul."**
>
> **Horace, The Epistles**

Araco (Laguardia, Alavesa, ☎ 941 600 209, 🖷 941 600 007), founded in 1986, is noted for its typical Basque architecture, while inside are modern facilities and state-of-the art technology. Araco have 200ha (494 acres) of vineyards making good red, white and rosé in the *joven* style under the *Señorío de Araco* label. Tempranillo and Viura grapes are used for the reds, 100 per cent Tempranillo for the rosé and 100 per cent Viura for the white. Group visits are by appointment.

Araex is a group of nine bodegas established in 1993, selling Riojan wines under various labels. These include *Don Balbino, Luis Cañas*, an excellent *reserva* (90 per cent Tempranillo, 5 per cent Viura and a 5 per cent mix of Graciano and Mazuelo) that is capable of benefiting from ageing in bottle for ten years or more, *Bodega Larchago, Heredad de Baroja, Muriel, Solaguen, Valserrano, Viña Diezmo* and *Lur*.

Arco Bodegas Unidas (see **Berberana Bodegas**).

Arca de Noé Coop Bodega (San Asensio, Alta, ☎/🖷 941 457 231) was founded in 1952 and has 101 barrels. Labels used include *Don Paulin*, *Monte San Quilez* and *Davalillo*, mainly for *joven* wines. No appointments are necessary for individuals or groups, with daily tastings mornings and afternoons (1.30 to 3pm is best avoided), except Sundays.

Ayale Lete Hijos, Ramón (Briñas, Alta, ☎/🖷 941 322 212) is over 100 years old, with a new bodega built in 1985. The 440m² (4,736ft²) underground cellars are cut into stone and contain 200 barrels, plus a number of modern stainless steel tanks. Ayale have 20ha (49 acres) of vineyards. Their excellent full flavoured *joven*, *crianza* and *reserva* wines are labelled *Viña Santurnia* and made from a blend of Tempranillo, Garnacha and Viura. Visits (individuals and groups) are daily (except Sundays) by appointment before 5pm and can be made at *Restaurante Bodegón Ayalain* in the village.

Balbino Fernandez Palacios (Lapuebla de Labarca, Alavesa, ☎/🖷 941 107 018) is a bodega where four generations have dedicated themselves to producing quality wines from 30ha (74 acres) and 1,200 barrels. All four approved red grapes and some white Viura are used in the red *Don Balbino crianza*, *reserva* and *gran reserva* wines. Visits are by appointment.

Barón de Ley (Mendavia, Baja, ① 948 694 303, ☎ 948 694 304) was founded in 1985 by *Bodegas El Coto* and is regarded as the leading bodega in the Rioja Baja, with ultra-modern installations and some 3,000 French oak barrels. It is an exciting, modern-style, single-estate producer using only its own grapes, mainly Tempranillo, although some Cabernet Sauvignon is also grown. The headquarters are located in a faithfully restored 16th century Benedictine monastery (a designated artistic monument) in the middle of a 90ha (220 acres) vineyard. Barón de Ley produce excellent, well-balanced wines, with the *reserva* being particularly smooth, elegant and rich tasting. Weekday visits are by appointment for individuals and groups. There is a shop and English and French are spoken.

Barón de Oña (Páganos – Laguardia, Alavesa) was sold in 1995 to the Haro *Bodegas La Rioja Alta*. See *Torre de Oña Bodegas*.

Bauza Bodega (Elciego, Alavesa, ① 941 606 216) is a fairly new bodega founded in 1985, with 12ha (30 acres) of vineyards and 105 barrels. Visits are daily (individuals and groups) by appointment.

Baigorri Anguiano, Jesús (Villabuena, Alavesa, ① 941 141 116, ☎ 941 135 865) was formed in 1980, although the bodega was originally founded at the turn of the century. A new building was constructed in 1980, uniquely with tanks coated with epoxy resin for optimum preservation of the wines. Carbonic maceration is used for the red *sin crianza*, which is produced from Tempranillo and Viura grapes. Individual and group visits are daily by appointment.

Berberana (Cenicero, Alta, ① 941 453 100, ☎ 941 453 114) was founded in Ollauri in 1877 by Martinez Berberana. The bodega is grandiose and one of the largest and most modern in Rioja with a huge ageing floor containing 30,000 barrels. The group was recently re-named *Arco Bodegas Unidas* and includes *Berberana, Lagunilla, Bodegas Hispano Argentinas, Marqués de Grinon, Marqués de Monistrol* and *Viñicola del Mediterraneo*.

Their wines include *Carta de Plata* red, a fruity *crianza* (the white *Carta de Plata* has no barrel ageing) and *Carta de Oro* white, which receives six months in barrel and has more body than the *Carta de Plata*. There is also a pleasant *Carta de Plata* rosé. The red **Carta de Oro** *crianza* has longer in oak (24 months*)* than most *crianzas* and is fuller and more mature tasting, while the **Berberana** *reservas* and *gran reservas* are quality reds with plenty of vanilla. **Preferido** is the label for a red *sin crianza* made from 60 per cent Tempranillo and 40 per cent Garnacha, plus a white and a rosé. **Dragon Tempranillo** is a young, modern-style red with a good mix of fruit and oak. Other names in the group are **Bodegas Mariscol, Viña Arisabel, Viña Canda, Viña Mara** and **Bodegas de Abalos** (a subsidiary). Group visits are by appointment.

Berceo, Bodegas (Haro, Alta, ☎ 941 310 744, 🖷 948 670 259) was founded in 1872 and is owned by the Gurpegui family. One of the oldest bodegas in the heart of Haro, it is the only remaining vertical one left, tastefully restored with an impressive electric carousel driving press-baskets on small railway trucks. Wooden fermentation vats were installed in 1983 to retain the character of the bodega. The cellars, dug into the hillside and dating from the Middle Ages, contain 3,800 barrels, 40 per cent in French oak. Berceo own 35ha (86 acres) of vineyards.

Gonzalo de Berceo *gran reserva* (only made in excellent years) and **Viña Berceo** *reserva*, made from Tempranillo, Mazuelo and Graciano, both good reliable reds, while the **Viña Berceo** *crianza* (made without the Mazuelo) can be excellent. The Gurpegui family owns a bodega in San Adrían (where the Rioja Baja overlaps Navarra) and the **Bodegas y Viñedos de la Plana** in Andosilla. Visits for individuals and groups are by appointment (French is spoken).

Beronia, Bodegas (Ollauri, Alta, ☎ 941 338 000, 🖷 941 338 266) is owned by Gonzalez Byass of sherry and brandy fame, and is a small modern bodega of traditional Riojan design. The 7.5ha (19 acres) of vineyards are in a natural setting in one of the best areas of Rioja Alta. Grapes and wine are also bought-in to produce reds in traditional oak style (while taking advantage of modern technology), which are aged in 7,000 barrels. The **Beronia** labelled wines are elegant and supple (made from 85 per cent Tempranillo, 7 per cent Mazuelo, 5 per cent Garnacha and 3 per cent Viura) and have an abundance of vanilla/wood taste. The whites are made by carbonic maceration and have what is now called 'modern freshness', together with a hint of exotic fruits. Visits are by appointment on weekdays for individuals and groups. English and French are spoken.

Berrueco Pérez, Jesús y José Antonio (Villabuena, Alavesa, ☏ 941 609 034) was founded in 1886 and still uses traditional winemaking techniques in an Alavesa-style bodega. They have 25ha (62 acres) of vineyards and 125 barrels in cellars cut from solid rock, complete with dining facilities and an old press. They make reliable, very fruity and full of taste *jóvenes* and *crianzas* using the ***Berrueco*** label. Appointments are unnecessary for daily visits (mornings and afternoons) by individuals and groups.

Berzal Otero, Jose Ramon y Hno (Baños de Ebro, Alava, ☏ 941 609 037) was founded in 1970 and is a modern bodega in the centre of town with 18ha (44 acres) of vineyards and both stainless steel and concrete tanks. Daily visits by individuals and groups are by appointment. They have a shop and English is spoken.

Bilbaínas, Bodegas (Haro, Alta, ☏ 941 310 147, ✉ 941 310 706) was founded in 1901 and the bodega was built at the then newly-opened railway link with Bilbao. The main building dates from the 19th century and is constructed in cut stone with a unique facade, while other buildings date from 1880, 1890, 1901 and 1971. There are over 1,000m² of underground wine cellars in cut stone – the most extensive in Rioja. Bilbaínas is a large bodega (recently purchased by ***Codorniú***) with 13,000 barrels and 250ha (617 acres) of vineyards, mostly around Haro, with a smaller holding at Leza in Rioja Alavesa.

They produce a wide range of reliable wines including the full bodied, plummy ***Viña Pomal*** *reserva* and *gran reserva*, using all four official red grape varieties, with grapes mainly from Leza. It is claimed that both Winston Churchill and Salvador Dali were fond of *Viña Pomal*, which is served at the Spanish court – if you like the taste of really good, aged Rioja you will certainly enjoy the *gran reserva*. ***Viña Zaco*** *reserva* is lighter, made without the Mazuelo, while the older vintages of ***Vendemia*** *especial reservas* are excellent and ***Gran Zaco*** is a full-bodied, quality, red *reserva* that ages well.

The delicious ***La Vicalanda de Viña Pomal*** *reserva 1994* (100 per cent Tempranillo) is of intense colour, full-bodied and with a wonderful aromatic bouquet of raspberry and liquorice, and a long finish. There is also a dry white Viura, **Viña Paceta**, and a Malvasía white labelled **Brillante**, a sweeter **Cepa de Oro**, a young red **Viña Ederra** crianza, plus a Cava sparkling wine, **Royal Carlton**. The **Imperator** label is used for the simple (un-aged) red, white and rosé wines. Bilbaínas welcome individual visitors on weekdays by appointment (English and French are spoken).

Biurko Gorri (Bargota, Baja, ☎ 948 648 370, ⊟ 948 648 370) was founded in 1992 in a partially buried stone, concrete and oak building, complete with 350 barrels and a rustic barbecue! Historically, the town of Bargota is famous for the 'Wizard of Bargota', Joannes de Bargota. Group visits are by appointment between 11am and 2pm and from 4 to 7pm.

Bodegas de Abalos (Ollauri, Alta, ☎ 941 453 100, ⊟ 941 454 537) was founded in 1691 and has 50ha (124 acres) of vineyards, 1,600 barrels as well as stainless steel fermentation tanks. They produce a **Bodegas de Abalos** red gran reserva containing 85 per cent Tempranillo, 10 per cent Mazuelo and 5 per cent Graciano, while their red and white crianzas are labelled **Viñedos D'Ávalos**.

Bodegas y Bebidas, formerly called **Savin**, is one of the largest Spanish wine producers with a controlling interest in **AGE**, **Campo Viejo** and **Marqués del Puerto**. See these entries for information.

Bodegas Bretón (Logroño, Alta, ☎ 941 212 225, ⊟ 941 211 098), founded in 1985, is built from pre-fabricated blocks. Their oenologist, Miguel Angel de Gregorio, and his enthusiastic team produce a good range of modern-style, intensely fruity **Loriñon** from their low-yielding 40ha (99 acres) of vineyards. The 1996 crianza received 15 months in oak and the reserva two years in oak followed by two in bottle. They also have another 20ha (49 acres) of vineyards for the expensive and excellent **Dominiò de Conte**, crianza, reserva and gran reserva, made from 85 per cent Tempranillo, 10 per cent Mazuelo and 5 per cent Graciano.

The 100 per cent Viura white **Loriñon** is a well-balanced, full-bodied, dry and fruity wine, with a hint of vanilla from the new American oak barrels. The majority of the 5,000 barrels are American oak, although the **Alba de Bretón** reserva 1995 uses very old (around 80 years) Tempranillo vines to produce a limited quantity of this exceptional red wine, which is aged for 26 months in new French Allier oak and American oak, followed by an additional couple of months in American oak. Daily visits (except Sundays) are by appointment for individuals and groups. English and French spoken.

Bodegas Burgo Viejo (Alfaro, Baja, ☎ 941 183 705, 🖷 941 183 405, ✉ bviejo@arrakis.es) was founded in 1964 and has 200ha (494 acres) of vineyards and 210 barrels. The bodega has an impressive chamber with the fermentation tanks rising up to the vaulted roof. Visits for individuals and groups are by appointment on weekday mornings and afternoons, except in August. There is a shop and they speak English and French.

Bodegas Gailur (Baños de Ebro, Alavesa, ☎ 941 109 158, 🖷 941 835 952) was formed in 1988 and has 101 barrels as well as stainless steel tanks. They produce a red Tempranillo *crianza* labelled *Ardanegi* plus *joven* red, white and rosé under the label *Solar Gailur*. Visits are by appointment.

Bodegas Guía Real (San Asensio, Alta, ☎ 941 457 578, 🖷 941 457 451) was founded in 1991 and has 300 barrels. They produce red *reserva*, *crianza* and *joven* wines using Tempranillo, Garnacha and Mazuelo under the *Vizconde de Uzqueta* label, together with a *Guía Real reserva* using the same grapes. Bodegas Guía Real produce another two ranges of *joven* red, white and rosé wines using the labels *Conde Albalat* and *Viña Eneldo*. Visits are by appointment.

Bodegas La Rioja Alta (Haro, Alta, ☎ 941 310 346, 🖷 941 312 854) was founded in 1890 when five vineyard-owning families formed the company. It is still a family-owned firm upholding the best Riojan winemaking traditions, while keeping up with modern practices and maintaining their dedication to quality. They have 300ha (741 acres) of vineyards and 30,000 barrels, and keep around nine years of wine in the bodega to ensure consistent high quality. Although employing the latest technology, their classical wines are still racked by hand and fined with egg whites, and attract high prices.

Viña Alberdi is a very good *crianza*, actually meeting *reserva* standards, made with 80 per cent Tempranillo, plus Graciano and Mazuelo, with two years in barrel (the first in new oak) followed by two years in bottle. It has lovely bold flavours with hints of vanilla. *Viña Arana* is an elegant *reserva*, often described as *Rioja Claret,* dry, fruity and long-lived. It is made mainly from Tempranillo (90 per cent), plus Graciano, Mazuelo and Viura, with three years in barrel and two in bottle. The red *Viña Ardanza* is an elegant and complex *reserva* that ages well, with spicy, intense, full-rounded, smooth richness, made from a blend of Tempranillo, 25 per cent Garnacha (giving the full body), Graciano and Mazuelo. It matures for 42 months in barrel and 30 months in bottle, and has a long balsamic finish.

The white *Viña Ardanza* is a traditional Riojan Viura white, needing good years, such as 1994, to produce aromatic, complex wine, which deserves to be more popular. The red *Gran Reserva 890* is made from 85 per cent Tempranillo, Graciano, Mazuelo and Viura, and is a distinctive, elegant, velvety wine with eight years in barrel and six in bottle. The red *Gran Reserva 904* is only made in excellent years after careful selection, of which the 1982 is a good example. After spending six years in American oak and four years in bottle, it is a superb example of Rioja Alta red wine at its best, made from 85 per cent Tempranillo, plus Mazuelo and Viura, but no Graciano. It has a bright, brick-red colour and a touch of gold, complete with a complex, harmonious character and long finish. It is also available in magnums, which mature more slowly than the standard bottle.

The white *Viña Ardanza reserva*, Viura plus a little Malvasía, is dry with a complex bouquet and full flavour with a hint of vanilla. *Marqués de Haro* red *gran reserva* is produced to mark special occasions, and for the year 2000 a double magnum bottle (3 litres) was produced. In addition to Tempranillo, Graciano and Mazuelo, it also contains 15 per cent Viura. Bodegas La Rioja Alta also own *Torre de Oña* at Páganos, which produces the new-style *Baron de Oña*. Weekday visits (mornings only) are by appointment for individuals and groups (English is spoken).

Bodegas de la Marquesa, see also *SMS Bodega, Vinedos y Bodegas de la MarquesA (Bodegas de Crianza SMS)*, is a small family concern producing limited quantities of excellent quality *crianza*, *reserva* and *gran reserva* **Valserrano**, mainly Tempranillo with a touch of Mazuelo and Graciano, aged in

American oak. Recent new wines include an excellent 100 per cent Graciano and a fruity white. All wines are made exclusively from the bodega's own grapes.

Bodegas de la Real Divisa (Abalos, Alta, ☎ 941 334 118, 🖷 941 258 155) was founded in 1968, although the main stone building including the façade dates back to the 12th century and their ancient stone caves contain 1,000 barrels of American oak. The building was originally one of the oldest bodegas in Europe and has the white lilies of the Royal House of Navarra above the main door. They have 35ha (86 acres) of vineyards and specialise in consistently good, oak-aged red wines, using grapes from their own vineyards. The *Marqués de Legarda gran reserva* and *reserva* have a good balance of fruit, wood and spices, and the *crianza* is also well made. The *joven* red is labelled *Real Divisa*. Visits are daily by appointment for individuals and groups, although weekends are preferred. English and French are spoken

Bodegas Tobía, *Provir* (San Asensio, Alta ☎ 941 547 425, 🖷 941 547 401) is a small, quality bodega of 25ha (62 acres), with 125 barrels of American oak. They produce young wines and *crianza* in limited quantities using modern equipment and great care. The bodega has its own restaurant, *La Bodega*, and visits are welcome between 8am and 10pm.

Bodegas y Viñas Senda Galiana (Villamediana de Iregua, Baja, ☎ 941 435 375, 🖷 941 451 005) was established in 1992. They produce a well-rounded *crianza*, *reserva* and *gran reserva* using 85 per cent Tempranillo, 10 per cent Garnacha and 5 per cent Mazuelo, labelled *Senda Galiana*, together with a fruity *joven* range under the *Mendiondo* label.

Campillo, Bodegas (Laguardia, Alavesa, ☎ 941 600 826, 🖷 941 600 837) is associated with *Bodegas Faustino Martinez,* having started life as their second label and used to 'break in' Faustino's new barrels. In 1990, Faustino launched Campillo as a new bodega producing light, quality red wines using the Tempranillo grape. They have 25ha (62 acres) of vineyards and 7,000 oak barrels, a quarter French. Campillo buy in Cabernet Sauvignon and make a good *reserva especial* using 40 per cent Cabernet Sauvignon and 60 per cent Tempranillo. Weekday visits are by appointment for individuals and groups. English, French and German are spoken.

Campo Burgo (Alfaro, Baja, ☎ 941 180 124, 📠 941 180 093) was founded in 1889 and has undergone a number of name changes over the years. This medium-sized bodega has buildings dating from the early 1900s made from 80cm (31in) thick, sun-dried bricks, mortar walls and wooden ceilings, and is surrounded by 15ha (37 acres) of vineyards and gardens. It uses bought-in grapes, some 80 per cent from Rioja Alta and the remainder from Rioja Baja. The large cellar areas contain around 4,000 barrels, 500 of French oak.

The *Campo Burgo* name is used on the labels for red *joven, crianza*, *reserva* and *gran reserva* wines made from Tempranillo and Garnacha grapes. The *reservas* can be very rounded and elegant with a subtle oakiness. The white is Viura, while the rosé is Garnacha and Tempranillo. *Viña Hermosa, Viña Lombas* and *Viña Algodi* labels are also used and contain the same grape varieties as Campo Burgo. Individual visits are weekdays and English, French and Dutch are spoken. Alfaro is a 1,000-year-old city boasting the largest colony of white storks in the world on a single building – so take an umbrella!

Campo Viejo, Bodegas (Logroño, Alta, ☎ 941 279 900, 📠 941 279 901) was founded in 1961 with *Bodegas y Bebidas* having a controlling interest, and is one of the largest firms in Rioja. They have 470ha (1,161 acres) of vineyards and 45,000 oak barrels (80 per cent American oak with the remainder French) housed in 15,000m² (over 160,000ft²) of ageing cellars. *Campo Viejo* has a well-earned reputation for good value wines. Their biggest seller, *San Asensio*, is a young *sin crianza* red, while *Albor* is another big seller, an inexpensive red made by carbonic maceration (they also produce a white *Albor*). Other wines include *Marqués de Villamagna* reserva and *gran reserva* – big fruity red Riojas produced only in the very best years – and a barrel-fermented white, *Viña Alcorta*, plus a *crianza* and *reserva* under the same label. The *Selección José Bezares* range includes a fruity red Tempranillo *crianza*, together with a Viura white and a Garnacha rosé. Individual visits on weekdays (English and French are spoken).

Cardema Bodegas (Fuenmayor, Alta, ☎/📠 941 451 083,) was founded in 1993, although the bodega was built in 1973.

They have 20ha (49 acres) of vineyards. Visits for individuals and groups are weekday mornings and afternoons. English is spoken.

Carlos Serres (Haro, Alta, ℗ 941 310 294, ☎ 941 310 418) was founded in 1896 and since 1987 has been owned by the Monthisa Group. Their wines are made using the traditional method and become more interesting with ageing in the bodega's 3,000 barrels. The *Carlos Serres crianza* contains 80 per cent Tempranillo and 20 per cent Garnacha, while the *gran reserva*, with 5 per cent less Garnacha, is well rounded. There is also a *joven* with 10 per cent Viura added. The superior *Onomástica reserva* is more complex, having been aged for three years in American oak. Other labels include the *Carlomagno reserva*, a *joven* 100 per cent Viura white, *Viña Marysol*, and *Cinco Barricas crianza*. Weekday visits for individuals and groups (English and French are spoken).

Casa Juan, Bodegas (Laguardia, Alavesa, ℗/☎ 941 121 241) was founded in an old flourmill by the Arbulu family during the first half of the 20th century. The main building has preserved its original coffered ceiling and brown oak posts, and contains a museum of equatorial African art above the underground cellars. The bodega was expanded in the '50s and has 15ha (37 acres) of vineyards and 200 barrels. Daily visits for individuals and groups (French is spoken).

Casado Fuertes, Herminio (Lapuebla de Labarca, Alavesa, ℗/☎ 941 607 017) was founded in 1980, although it has ancient underground cellars (8m/26ft deep) with stone arches containing 35 barrels. The bodega has 30ha (74 acres) of vineyards. Visits for individuals and groups are daily, mornings and afternoons, by appointment. English, French and German are spoken.

Casado Fuertes, Luis (Lapuebla de Labarca, Alavesa, ℗/☎ 941 607 001) was founded in 1970 and is an old bodega with concrete fermentation pools and tanks, 500 barrels and 30ha (74 acres) of vineyards. They use the *Jaun de Alzate* label for their good quality aged wines up to *gran reserva*, which contain a blend of 88 per cent Tempranillo, 7 per cent Viura and 5 per cent Graciano. The *Covara* label is used for a *joven* red, white and rosé. Visits for individuals and groups on weekdays are by appointment.

Casado Manzanos, Luis Angel (Lapuebla de Labarca, Alavesa, ① 941 127 556, ✆ 941 127 256) was founded in 1991 in a bodega built in 1942 with stone floors, Arabic-tiled roofs, and fermentation pools and tanks made from concrete and stainless steel. Casado Manzanos have 12ha (30 acres) of vineyards and 115 barrels, and produce very good red *joven* and *crianza* (in limited quantities) labelled *Jilabá*. Visits for individuals and groups are daily by appointment. There is a shop and dining room, and both English and French are spoken.

Casado Morales (Lapuebla de Labarca, Alava, ① 941 607 017) was founded in 1983 and is a small bodega with 25ha (62 acres) of vineyards producing good reds and rosé using the traditional grape varieties.

Castillo de Cuzcurrita (Cuzcurrita de Rio Tiron, Alta, ① 941 301 620, ✆ 941 151 071) is a small bodega housed in a 14th century castle and gardens, surrounded by 12ha (30 acres) of vineyards. Since 1945 it has been the family home of the Count of Alacha who has restored it beautifully and added new buildings in the original style. The bodega was founded in 1971 and has 600 barrels, which are stored in the old tower. They produce interesting wood-aged red wines from their own vineyards under the labels of *Castillo de Cazcurrita crianza* and *Conde de Alacha reserva* (both 100 per cent Tempranillo).

Castillo de Fuenmayor (Fuenmayor, Alta, ① 941 450 387, ✆ 941 451 005) produce *Blasón de Esquide gran reserva* and *reserva* reds using all four of Rioja's official red grapes, while the *crianza* is made from Tempranillo, Garnacha and Graciano. *Gardingo* and *Cepa Tintana* labels are used for their *joven* ranges.

Castillo de Ygay, see Bodegas Marqués de Murrieta.

Castresana Bodegas (Tirgo, Alta, ① 941 301 684) was founded in 1992 and has 25ha (62 acres) of vineyards and 300 barrels. Visits for individuals and groups are daily by appointment. French is spoken.

Compañía Internacional de Vinos (Cenicero, Alta) is a subsidiary of *Bodegas Montecillo,* which in turn is owned by *Osborne*. Wines are exclusively for export and they also use bought-in wines, with *Brigadier Miranda* their main label.

Compañía Vinícola del Norte de España (Haro, Alta, ① 941 304 800, ✆ 941 304 815), known by its initials, CVNE, (pronounced 'Coo-nay', as if the 'V' was an 'E'), was founded in 1879 and in 1989 invested heavily in a new winery. They have 19th century warehouses and cellars, and an 1895 Malvoisin pasteuriser. CVNE is owned by the Real de Asúa family and is one of the leading Rioja bodegas with 550ha (1,359 acres) of vineyards and 25,000 barrels, 30 per cent in French oak. Under the *Cune* label there is a reliable red *crianza, Cune Rioja Clarete,* with 70 per cent Tempranillo, 20 per cent Garnacha tinto, 5 per cent Graciano and a 5 per cent blend of Viura and Garnacha Blanca, and *Cune reserva*, a 100 per cent Viura white and a 100 per cent rosé Garnacha *tinto*. The excellent red *Imperial* is a very smooth wine made from the best selection from the best years, produced as both a *reserva* and *gran reserva,* and also a plummier, fuller *Viña Real crianza, reserva* and *gran reserva.*

The *Monopole* is a superb white. CVNE also produce a new-style white Rioja, *Cune Lanceros*, without wood-ageing, and *Corona*, a semi-sweet white from 70 per cent Viura and a 30 per cent blend of Garnacha Blanca and Malvasía. They produce a wide range of Riojan wines in both Rioja Alavesa and Rioja Alta styles, with the single-vineyard red, *Contino*, (from La Serna, west of Oyón in Rioja Alavesa), just one of their many fine wines. All of these worthy, full-bodied, mellow wines have a blackberry flavour and a characteristically long finish, and are excellent value. Visits for individuals and groups are by appointment on weekday mornings and afternoons (avoid 1 to 3pm). English, French and German are spoken.

Consejo de la Alta, Bodegas (Cenicero, Alta, ① 941 455 005, ✉ 941 455 010) have 25ha (62 acres) of vineyards and 700 barrels. The *Alta Río* label is used for their range of *joven* red, white, and rosé and red Tempranillo *crianza* wines, the latter matured in American oak barrels for 12 months and a minimum of nine months in bottle. It has an intense colour with a Tempranillo nose, is smooth, well-made and with a good finish. Visits are by appointment (closed in August).

Contino (Laguardia, Alavesa), now a subsidiary of **CVNE**, was founded in 1974 and is a good, single vineyard red *reserva* with two years in barrel and two in bottle. The bodega has 45ha (111 acres) of vineyards planted around a 17th century manor.

The wines typically contain 85 per cent Tempranillo and are aged in French rather than American oak.

CooP Cal de Navarette (Navarette, Alta, ➀/🖷 941 440 626) has 333ha (822 acres) of vineyards. It produces various ranges of *jóvenes* using **Abadía de Altillo**, **Campo Babiero**, **Heredad de Altillo** and **Vega Vizcaino** labels. The red wines contain Tempranillo and Mazuelo, the white is Viura and the rosé Tempranillo and Viura. Visits are by appointment from Mondays to Saturdays.

Corral Bodegas (Navarette, Alta, ➀ 941 440 193, 🖷 941 440 195), founded in 1898, is a well-respected, family-owned bodega situated on the *Pilgrims' Way* and next to the ruins of the *Hospice of San Juan de Acre*, although in 1974 the old bodega moved to its current location. Corral have 40ha (99 acres) of vineyards and 5,000 barrels of American, French and, unusually, Yugoslav oak. They produce good classic Riojas of improving quality. The **Don Jacobo** label is used for a red *crianza*, *reserva*, *joven* white and rosé, while **Corral** is a very good *gran reserva* containing 80 per cent Tempranillo, 15 per cent Garnacha and 5 per cent Mazuelo. The fresh, white *joven* contains 100 per cent Viura. Visits for both individuals and groups are by appointment all day from Mondays to Saturdays and Sunday mornings. English, French and German are spoken.

El Coto, Bodegas (Oyon, Alavesa, ➀ 941 122 216, 🖷 941 111 015) was founded in 1973 and has a cellar of over 12,000 barrels. It is best known for its soft, light red **El Coto** *crianza* and **Coto de Imaz** *reserva* and *gran reserva*, all of which are well-balanced, stylish 100 per cent Tempranillo. **Coto Mayor** is a red *reserva*, also 100 per cent Tempranillo. Individual visits are by appointment from Mondays to Thursdays (English is spoken).

Cosecheros Alaveses (Laguardia, Alavesa, ➀ 941 600 119, 🖷 941 600 850) was founded in 1985 by six independent producers and re-formed as a private concern in 1992. They produce distinctive modern-style Riojas and are best known for their outstanding, un-oaked red, well-balanced and fruity **Artadi**, and they also make excellent 100 per cent Tempranillo *crianzas* and *reservas*. **Artadi Pagos Viejos** *reserva* has great elegance and complexity, and is one of Rioja's most expensive wines, being produced from vines over 50 years old and in limited quantities only. Cosecheros Alaveses have 70ha (173 acres) of vineyards around Laguardia and 1,000 barrels, a quarter in French oak. Other labels used are *Viña el Pison*, *Viñas de Gain*, *Valdepomares* and *Orobio*. The main *Viña Artadi* is red, but they also produce a good white (100 per cent Viura) and a 100 per cent Garnacha rosé. Individual and group visits are on weekdays (English and French are spoken).

Cosecheros de Tudelilla (Tudelilla, Baja, ☉/☎ 941 152 131) was founded in 1991 with modern facilities and 98ha (242 acres) of vineyards. Individual and group visits are daily, including the old bodega, both mornings and afternoons (closed from 1 to 2pm).

Domecq Bodegas (Elciego, Alavesa, ☉ 941 606 001, ☎ 941 606 235) was founded in 1973 by the famous sherry company when it purchased over 400ha (1,000 acres) of vineyards in Rioja Alavesa. Modern stainless steel fermentation tanks were installed along with 21,000 barrels and a system was developed to give the Alavesa wines more colour than usual. The vines are trellis-trained in the Bordeaux style, rather than the lower *en vaso* Riojan method, and although the bodega is huge, grapes and wines still need to be bought-in. The reliable *Viña Eguia crianza* is 90 per cent Tempranillo and a 10 per cent blend of Garnacha, Graciano and Mazuelo, while the older, refined *Marqués de Arienzo gran reserva* is 100 per cent Tempranillo. The red *reserva* and *crianza* are 95 per cent Tempranillo, Graciano and Mazuelo, and the white 100 per cent Viura. Restricted visits are by appointment, Mondays to Fridays from 10am until 2pm.

Domínguez Fernández, Eduardo C (Briñas, Alta, ☉ 941 312 226) are situated 3km outside Haro and produce very good *crianzas* and *reservas* labelled *Mentoste*. The other label used, *Vendigorna*, is for the *joven* red containing the same blend of grapes as the *Mentoste* wines (60 per cent Tempranillo, 20 per cent Garnacha, 10 per cent Mazuelo and 10 per cent Viura). Visits by appointment.

Escudero, *Provir* (Gravalos, Baja ☉ 941 398 008, ☎ 941 398 070), founded in 1852, is a small family-owned bodega, and the second bodega in Rioja to make Cava, which it now produces from its own Chardonnay grapes. They have 70ha (173 acres) of vineyards and 360 barrels. Escudero produce good to very good quality reds, including *Becquer Primicia*, a 100 per cent Garnacha, and *Solar de Becquer* crianza and *reserva* containing 60 per cent Tempranillo and 20 per cent each of Garnacha and Mazuelo. There is also a *Heredad Bienzoval joven* red, white and rosé, and *Benito Escudero Abad (BEA)* Cava. Individual and group visits are by appointment daily from 9am to 6pm. English and French are spoken.

Estraunza, Bodegas (Lapuebla de Labarca, Alavesa, ① 941 127 245, ✆ 941 127 293) was founded in 1991 and has 30ha (74 acres) of vineyards and 635 barrels. They buy in ready made wines which are aged in-house, the best of which is *Solar de Estraunza* crianza and *reserva*. They also produce *joven* white and rosé, and *Superbe*, a red *joven* made from 100 per cent Tempranillo. Daily visits are by appointment for individuals and groups.

Faustino Martínez (Oyón, Alavesa, ① 941 122 100, ✆ 941 122 106) was founded in 1861, with the current bodega being built in 1930. It is a family firm with around 500ha (1,235 acres), in one of the best lime-clay areas of Rioja Alavesa, and owns 5,000 barrels. They produce consistently good wines, mainly using Tempranillo in both old and new styles, with little oak ageing. The *gran reserva Faustino 1*, for example, spends just two years in barrel with the remainder in bottle. The reliable red *Faustino V reserva* is 85 per cent Tempranillo and 15 per cent Graciano and the white *Faustino V* is a delicately, oak-aged Viura of excellent quality.

The wines are bottled in characteristic, frosted, antique-style bottles, with fine art labels of painters and musicians such as Rembrandt, El Greco and Gluck. *Faustino VII* is a less complex but reliable *joven* range – the red is made by carbonic maceration with 95 per cent Tempranillo and 5 per cent Mazuelo, and has a dark plum colour and blackberry bouquet, while the rosé is 100 per cent Garnacha. *Bodegas Campillo* (Laguardia) is a subsidiary as is the *Señor Burgués* brand name. Individual and group visits are on weekdays, although you need to make an appointment at least two weeks in advance. English, French and German are spoken.

Faustino Rivero Ulecia (Arnedo, Baja, ① 941 380 057, ✆ 941 380 156) have 2,000 barrels and use bought-in grapes. The

Faustino Rivero Ulecia label has a full range of reds up to *gran reserva*, which use Tempranillo, Mazuelo and Graciano grapes, together with a *joven* white and rosé. The simple **Rasillo** red is made from 30 per cent Tempranillo and 70 per cent Garnacha, the *crianza* **Chitón** has a more obvious wood and vanilla flavour and contains 50 per cent Tempranillo, while the **Señorio de Prayla** *reserva* has 70 per cent Tempranillo. The **Rasillo** rosé is fresh and fruity. Weekday visits (mornings and afternoons) are by appointment for individuals and groups. English and French are spoken.

Fernández de Manzanos, *Provir* (Aldeanuevo de Ebro, Baja ①/☎ 941 163 584) was founded in 1927. The bodega is built in traditional Riojan style with underground cellars containing 500 barrels of French and American oak, using modern technology. The *crianza*, **Viña Marichalar**, contains mainly Tempranillo plus some Mazuelo, while the white **Viña Berri** *joven* is Viura, and the rosé Garnacha and Viura. Visits by individuals and groups are by appointment and French is spoken.

Finca la Grajera (Logroño, Alta, ① 941 291 263, ☎ 941 251 606) was founded in 1977 and has 65ha (161 acres) of vineyards and 100 barrels. Visits by individuals and groups are by appointment from 8am to 4pm and can include the experimental plots of the Agricultural Research and Development Centre. English is spoken.

Florentino de Lecanda (Haro, Alta, ① 941 303 477) was founded in 1965 and is located in the town's traditional winemaking quarter. The bodega is designed in traditional Riojan style in natural stone and limestone and houses 650 barrels. Florentino are noted for their fine *reservas* made from 90 per cent Tempranillo and a 10 per cent blend of Garnacha, Mazuelo and Graciano, while the *crianza* is 100 per cent Tempranillo. Visits are by appointment on weekdays (mornings and afternoons) and English is spoken.

Florentino Martínez Rubio (Cordovin, Alta, ①/☎ 941 418 614) was founded in 1992 and is a new bodega with a red brick façade and wooden eaves, equipped with modern stainless steel tanks and a bottling plant. They own 14ha (35 acres) of vineyards. The *cosecheros jóvenes* are fresh and fruity, using **Valdeviñero** and **Florentino Martínez** labels. No appointments are necessary for weekday visits by individuals, which are from 10.30am to 1.30pm and from 4 to 7.30pm.

Franco-Españolas, Bodegas (Logroño, Alta, ① 941 251 300, ⌨ 941 262 948) was founded in 1890 and is now part of a company controlled by the *Marcos Eguizábel Group* (which includes *Federico Paternina* and some sherry houses). In 1890, the Frenchman Frederic Anglade arrived from Bordeaux to buy grapes in Logroño and purchased some land to set up his own wine business. The bodega, one of the historical bodegas favoured by royalty (Alfonso XII and XIII), is situated in a picturesque setting overlooking a bridge on the western bank of the River Ebro and has been lovingly maintained. The estate's vineyards have long since been sold and bought-in grapes are mainly used for the dozen or so wines currently produced, although the company still owns 54ha (133 acres) of vineyards and has 14,000 barrels housed in extensive underground cellars.

The pleasing *Rioja Bordón crianza* is a fruity, medium red which is also made as a *reserva* and *gran reserva*, and in exceptional years red *Excelso gran reserva* is made in small quantities using equal proportions of Tempranillo, Graciano and Mazuelo. The interesting *Centenario gran reserva* is a blend of 70 per cent Tempranillo, 15 per cent Graciano and 15 per cent Mazuelo. The semi-sweet white *Diamante* and the *Viña Soledad* white (100 per cent Viura), sold in slender brown bottles, are also popular. Also produced in exceptional years are *Viña Soledad reserva* and *Tête de Cuvée gran reserva*, using 50 per cent Viura, 25 per cent Malvasía and 25 per cent Garnacha Blanca, which is aged for four years, has a vanilla bouquet and a smooth, refined taste.

Viña Sole is a white *crianza*, *Castil Corvo* a *joven* white and *Rosé de Lujo* a *joven* rosé. Subsidiary brands are *Casa de la Reina, Conde Bel, Conde Lar* and the lightweight *Royal*. Individual and group visits are weekdays by appointment. There is a shop and English and French are spoken.

Galarza San Millán, Emiliano (Leza, Alavesa, ① 941 605 004) was founded in 1973 and is a single estate with a bodega built in traditional stone. They have 18ha (44 acres) of vineyards and 25 barrels. The production of the *Galarza* range of *joven* red, white and rosé is strictly controlled. Visits for individuals and groups are by appointment.

Garcia Berrueco, Juan José (Villabueno, Alavesa, ① 941 619 119) was founded in 1986 and is a modern building. They have 12ha (30 acres) of vineyards. No appointments are necessary for visits by individuals or groups.

Garcia Chávarri, Amador (Baños de Ebro, Alavesa, ① 941 121 322, ✉ 941 290 373) was founded in 1985 and the bodega is built in contemporary style with modern stainless steel tanks and has 6ha (15 acres) of vineyards. Individual and group visits are by appointment, mornings and afternoons except between 1 and 4pm. The bodega has a shop.

Garcia Viñegra, Juan Teófilo (Elvillar, Alavesa, ①/✉ 945 231 924) was founded in 1916 and visits by individuals and groups are by appointment. They have a shop.

Garrida Garcia, Eduardo (Abalos, Alta, ①/✉ 941 334 187) was founded in 1950 and the original stone house was renovated in 1987. They have 2ha (5 acres) of vineyards and 110 barrels. Daily visits by individuals and groups are by appointment and include a museum containing traditional viticultural and vinicultural objects. A tour of the village church and local mansions can also be arranged. English and French are spoken.

Gil Garcia, Santiago (Labastida, Alavesa, ① 941 331 292) was founded in 1992 with 20ha (49 acres) of vineyards. The bodega contains a 16th century cave (8m/26ft deep) hewn out of the rock and a stone fermentation pool. Individual and group tastings are by appointment from 10am to 1pm and 3 to 10pm.

If you spill red wine onto a carpet or your clothes, immediately pour white wine on the affected area and leave to dry (do not rub). You will be amazed that no red stain remains.

Gil Varela, José Angel y Otros (San Vicente de la Sonsierra, Alta, ① 941 334 471) was founded in 1993 and has 20ha (49 acres) of vineyards and 30 barrels. They produce a red *joven*, ***Viña Olmaza***, using 90 per cent Tempranillo, 5 per cent

Viura and 5 per cent Garnacha. Daily visits for individuals and groups are by appointment.

Gómez Cruzado (Haro, Alta, ① 941 312 502, ✉ 941 303 567) was founded in 1886 and the barrel-ageing chambers contain 2,000 barrels plus the original oak fermentation vats. Three labels are used: *Viña Dorana*, *Regio Honorable* and *Predilecto*, the latter for the *joven* red, white and rosé. The *Viña Dorana* gran reserva and reserva are 80 per cent Tempranillo and 20 per cent Mazuelo, while the very fruity crianza has 5 per cent less Mazuelo that is replaced by Graciano. The excellent red *Regio Honorable* gran reserva uses the same grapes as the *Viña Dorana* gran reserva. Individual and group visits are by appointment daily (except Sundays), mornings and afternoons. English is spoken.

Gurpegui Muga, Bodegas Luis (San Adrian, Baja, ① 948 670 050, ✉ 948 670 259) was founded in 1921 and has 100ha (247 acres) of vineyards, 8,000 barrels and a winemaking plant with thermal vinification. They also own the subsidiary firm, *Bodegas Berceo*, and were the first house in Rioja to produce rosé on a large scale – Luis Gurpegui is known locally as the 'king of rosé'. The majority of wine is made with bought-in wine and grapes, with great care taken to ensure that the resulting wine retains the character of the grapes used. The main label is *Viñadrian*, mainly *joven* with no barrel ageing, while some aged wines are from *Bodegas Berceo*. Subsidiary brand names are *Aplauso, Riazan* and *Don Quintiliano*. This go-ahead producer also makes Navarra wines and is certainly a bodega to watch. Visits by individuals and groups are by appointment on weekdays between 9am and 1.30pm. English and French are spoken.

Guzmán Alonso, Javier (Navaridas, Alavesa, ① 941 605 029) was founded in 1900 (the cellars have round arches and contain the old winemaking facilities) and has 18ha (44 acres) of vineyards and 80 barrels. The Renaissance house bears the ancient coat of arms, *Heredad Guzmán Aldazábal*, dating from 1700. The *joven*, *Javier Guzmán Aldazábal*, contains 85 per cent Tempranillo and 15 per cent Viura, and spends three to four months in barrel to give it more character. Individual and group visits are daily by appointment and include tastings and a commentary. The bodega also has a dining room that serves meals.

Heredad de Baroja (Elvillar, Alavesa, ➀ 941 604 068, ▭ 941 604 105), near Fuenmayor, was founded in 1988, with one of the bodega's buildings designed as a small reproduction castle. The 40ha (99 acres) of vineyards provide around 10 per cent of production, the rest consisting of bought-in wines. However, the bodega has 20,000 odd barrels, which allows more wine to be stored in oak than in the fermentation tanks – even the red *Baroja joven* is aged in wood, leading to a distinctive and unusual wine. *Viña Baroja* is made by carbonic maceration, while the *Rincón de Baroja crianza,* a juicy red, is produced from all four of Rioja's official red grapes and has lots of wood and vanilla. The *Heredad de Baroja gran reserva* and *reserva* also use all the red grape varieties plus 15 per cent Viura.

Heredad de Ugarte (Paganos, Alavesa, ➀ 941 126 043, ▭ 941 271 319) is situated 2km from Laguardia between two *dolmen*s – ancient burial mounds – named *Satillo* and *San Martín*. The bodega was founded in 1987 and is a unique cave (even the toilets are in a cave) with wonderful views of the Sierra de Cantabria mountains to the north and a balcony overlooking the Rioja Alavesa vineyards to the south. The bodega has 105ha (259 acres) of vineyards and 600 barrels. *Heredad Ugarte crianza* is typical of the house style, using 80 per cent Tempranillo and 20 per cent Garnacha, and aged for 18 months in American oak and eight months in bottle. Other labels include *Cédula Real gran reserva* (80 per cent Tempranillo and 20 per cent Garnacha), *Dominio de Ugarte reserva* and *crianza* (95 per cent Tempranillo, 5 per cent Garnacha), and *Término de Ugarte* and *Anade joven* red, white and rosé ranges. Visits for individuals and groups are by appointment from Mondays to Thursdays. There is a shop and English is spoken.

Herencia Lasanta (Laguardia, Alavesa, ➀ 941 121 234, ▭ 941 121 236) was founded in 1935 and produces very good red *joven, crianza*, *reserva* and *gran reserva* wines.

Hermanos Hurtado, Bodegas (Navarette, Alta, ➀ 941 440 031, ▭ 941 440 612) was founded in 1970 and uses bought-in grapes and wine, which they age in their 4,000 barrels. *Hurtado*

1 is a *gran reserva* made from 90 per cent Tempranillo, 5 per cent Graciano and 5 per cent Mazuelo, while the ***Hurtado*** label is also used for red *crianza* and *reserva*, and *joven* white, red and rosé. ***Viña Ironda*** and ***Viña Balgarauz*** are also ranges of *joven*, *crianza*, *reserva* and *gran reserva*. Individual and group visits are by appointment on weekdays. There is also a shop.

Hermanos Peciña, Bodegas (San Vicente de la Sonsierra, Alta, ℑ 941 334 133) was founded in 1997 and has 40ha (99 acres) of vineyards and 2,300 barrels. Individual and group visits are by appointment, mornings and afternoons. There is a shop and English is spoken.

Ilurce, Bodegas y Vinedos (Alfaro, Baja, ℑ/🖷 941 180 829) was founded in 1940 and has traditional Riojan architecture with 200-year-old ageing cellars located alongside a modern vinification plant complete with stainless steel tanks. They have 40ha (99 acres) of vineyards and 35 barrels. Visits are daily by appointment (individuals and groups) and there is a shop.

Jalón López, Francisco (Yecora, Alavesa, ℑ 941 601 130) was founded in 1970 and has 14ha (35 acres) of vineyards. Visits are daily by appointment (individuals and groups) and can be combined with a visit to the village to see its fountains, shrines and parks.

Lagunilla, Bodegas (Fuenmayor, Alta, ℑ 941 450 100, 🖷 941 450 186) was founded in 1885 and was the first to introduce American rootstock to combat the phylloxera plague. They use the labels of ***Lagunilla*** and ***Viña Herminia***, the latter a better buy, particularly the older vintages using 85 per cent Tempranillo and 15 per cent Garnacha. Wines are bought-in, blended and then aged in over 10,000 barrels.

Lan, Bodegas (Fuenmayor, Alta, ℑ 941 450 050, 🖷 941 450 567). The name 'LAN' comes from the initials of Logroño, Alava and Navarra, the three original 'Riojan' provinces, although Logroño is no longer a province. Established in 1970 and recently re-organised, Lan has a large modern bodega with 70ha (173 acres) of vineyards and 12,000 barrels. The youngest wines are sold as ***Lan***, including a fruity 100 per cent Garnacha rosé, and an excellent red *crianza*. The ***Lander*** wines (70 per cent Tempranillo, 25 per cent Mazuelo and 5 per cent Garnacha) are older vintages with more oak. ***Lanciano***, with less Mazuelo and more Garnacha, is more mature and oaky, elegant and clean tasting. ***Señorío de Ulla*** and ***Lancorta*** are subsidiary brands. Individual and group visits are on weekday mornings and afternoons (English is spoken).

Lapuebla Vinícola Coop (Lapuebla de Labarca, Alavesa, ✆ 941 127 232, ✉ 941 127 295) was founded in 1987 with 250ha (618 acres) of vineyards and 108 barrels. They have modern stainless steel tanks and use carbonic maceration with de-stalked grapes. Lapuebla produce two ranges of *joven* wines, ***Mesa Mayor*** and ***Covila***. Daily individual and group visits are by appointment.

Larrea Merino, Miguel Angel (Badaran, Alta, ✆ 941 367 393) was founded in 1930 and was one of the first bodegas constructed in cement with round arches (they also have six fermentation tanks from the turn of the century). The bodega has 6ha (15 acres) of vineyards. The label ***Miguel Angel Larrea Merino*** is used for their *joven* red, white and rosé wines. Visits, which include the vineyards, are organised by appointment on weekdays for individuals only (no groups). English is spoken.

Leza García, Bodegas (Uruñuela, Alta, ✆/✉ 941 371 045) is a small family bodega founded in 1980 with 15ha (37 acres) of vineyards. The bodega is a concrete structure, although it has traditional fermentation pools and underground storage caves. Leza García produce *joven* red, white and rosé of one or two years of age under the labels of ***Valdepalacios*** (75 per cent Tempranillo, 15 per cent Viura and 5 per cent each of Mazuelo and Garnacha) and ***Postural*** (80 per cent Tempranillo, 10 per cent Garnacha and 10 per cent Viura). Individual and group visits are on Saturdays only, from 10.30am to 6pm. English and French are spoken.

López Agos, Bodegas (see **Bodegas Marqués del Puerto**).

López de Heredia, Viña Tondonia Rioja (Haro, Alta, ✆ 941 310 244, ✉ 941 310 788) produces traditional, classical, long-lasting wines from this 'old fashioned and proud of it' bodega founded in 1877 at the height of the phylloxera epidemic in France. The bodega's distinctive tower dates from 1892 when a Chilean, Rafael López de Heredia, whose family still own the bodega, built cellars, offices and a lodge using quarried stone. The cellars are 17m (56ft) below ground, which helps to maintain an even 12°C. Entering the bodega is a journey back in time, with wooden fermentation vats still in use, wine transference done by hand in underground cellars black with mould, cobwebs in the tasting room, wines fined with egg whites and the tops of the bottles dipped in molten wax. The 15,000 or so barrels are mainly of American oak.

All wine is vinified by the bodega and its 162ha (about 400 acres) supplies around half of its grapes, with the remainder being bought-in. The house style is rich, oaked refinement, with wines made to last in the traditional style, ageing wonderfully well after their long period in oak. The younger red, *Viña Cubillo* crianza is stylish, the *Viña Bosconia* more mature, the *Viña Tondonia* reserva a splendidly elegant, well-balanced, rich red, and the *gran reserva* an established firmer classic. About a quarter of the wines are whites, which include a smooth, fresh *Viña Gravonia* and a more complex *Viña Tondonia* with a subtle blend of oak and fruit. If you think that aged white Riojas are flat and oxidised, prepare to be pleasantly surprised. Visits by appointment.

Luis Alegre, Bodegas (Laguardia, Alavesa, ☾/🖷 941 600 089) was founded in 1978 and is a family bodega originally situated inside a cave in Laguardia. The present bodega has 12ha (30 acres) of vineyards and is a modern construction with the latest equipment and 105 barrels, although the traditional style is maintained. Group visits by appointment (no individuals). English and French are spoken.

Luis Cañas, Bodegas (Villabuena, Alavesa, ☾ 941 123 373, 🖷 941 609 289, ✉ bodegas@luiscanas.com) was founded commercially in 1970, with modern facilities installed in the old bodega in 1994 (the family tradition dates back to a winery from 1928). The bodega has 24ha (59 acres) of vineyards with spectacular views and 1,250 barrels, 70 per cent French and 30 per cent American. Luis Cañas produce good, well balanced white, rosé and red wines, from *joven* to *gran reserva* using the *Luis Cañas* label, some of which have won international awards. All grape varieties are used, although 90 to 95 per cent Tempranillo is the basis, producing smooth, red fruit and vanilla wines. Visits (individuals and groups) are by appointment, weekday mornings and afternoons and Saturday mornings. The bodega is closed on Sundays and for the whole of August. English is spoken.

Maese Joan, Bodegas (Oyón, Alavesa, ☼/☎ 941 122 134) is owned by *Larios Gin* and was founded in 1989 in conjunction with over a dozen winegrowers who owned 170ha (420 acres) of vineyards. The latest equipment and technology is employed. The *joven* wines are labelled *Vinalzada* and the *crianza Armorial*, while other wood-aged wines are labelled *Vega Vieja*. The latter's *crianza* and *reserva* have a good combination of fruit (especially raspberries) and wood. *Coro Black Label* is a fruity red with some body having received two months wood ageing.

> **"Wine cureth the fiercest of woes."**
> **Graffito from Herculaneum**

Marín Díez, Luis (Fuenmayor, Alta, ☼ 941 630 024, ☎ 941 644 105), founded in 1991, is situated on the road between Fuenmayor and Logroño. They own just 4ha (10 acres) of vineyards with 132 barrels and strive to maintain the highest quality for their limited production, sold under the *Basape* and *Viña Asomante* labels. Visits are by appointment.

Marqués de Cáceres, Bodegas (Cenicero, Alta, ☼/☎ 941 454 000). At the end of the '60s, Don Enrique Forner, co-owner with his brother of a château in the Haut-Médoc in Bordeaux, established a bodega in Rioja. He enlisted the help of Professor Peynaud of Bordeaux University and together they decided on Cenicero due to the high quality of grapes grown there. The methods used have more in common with Bordeaux than Rioja and the resulting wines are less oaky in the modern style, with the wood balanced by the fruit. Sr. Forner believes in a shorter period in the barrel and a longer time maturing in bottle.

The *Marqués de Cáceres crianza, reserva* and *gran reserva* (85 per cent Tempranillo and a 15 per cent blend of Garnacha, Mazuelo and Graciano) are characterised by a balance of wood and blackberry fruit, with enough body to enable long ageing.

Under the same name are *joven* white and rosé and a *crianza* white (100 per cent Viura). There is not any ageing of the **Satinela** white and rosé wines. Marqués de Cáceres produce over half a million cases of quality wine annually and in order to ensure an adequate supply of grapes, the *Unión Viti-Vinícola de Logroño* was formed by 16 winegrowers to supply the grapes required. The growers are given precise instructions regarding the time to start picking and fermentation temperatures are carefully controlled.

Marqués de Cáceres was the first bodega to ferment white and rosé Rioja at low temperatures, producing lively, fresh, fruity wines. They have over 20,000 barrels, roughly split between French and American oak, with some Spanish oak barrels also used. Wines include two *crianza* whites, a 100 per cent Viura and a blend of 90 per cent Viura and 10 per cent Malvasía, both of which are clean, fresh and fruity with a touch of oak. Their red and white wines are characterised by a long finish. Other labels used are **Constanilla**, **Gran Vendema** and **Rivarey**. Visits by appointment.

Marqués de Griñón (Ollauri, Alta, ① 941 338 002, ✉ 941 453 114) was founded in 1994 as a joint venture with **Berberana**. It is a typical Riojan bodega with 200-year-old cellars containing 750 barrels. A range of red (only) *joven* to *reserva especial* are produced under the **Griñón** label in a modern, fruity, quality style, using the best Tempranillo grapes, with the wines being vinified separately. Individual and group visits are by appointment on weekdays (closed in August).

Marqués de Murrieta (Ygay, near Logroño, Alta, ① 941 258 100, ✉ 941 251 606), on the road to Zaragossa, was established in 1852 and their cellars created in 1872. The bodega consists of three stone buildings, the main building being the old Ygay castle, in an estate of 290ha (717 acres). They have 185ha (457 acres) of vineyards surrounding the historic buildings and 13,200 barrels. Murrieta are a much-respected bodega, the second bodega of the modern Rioja era together with **Marqués de Riscal**, the other great pioneer of Bordeaux-style winemaking. The founder, Luciano de Murrieta, was the first person to export Spanish wine in barrels. He was made a Marqués when he was 50 years old, a fitting and well-deserved birthday present, although the Bodega is now owned by the Cebrián family, *Condes* (counts) of Creixell.

The tradition has been to age the red wines for very long periods in oak, and until new regulations altered the practice, the wines were bottled immediately before shipping. It is a single-estate wine and well known for its high quality red **Castillo de Ygay** *gran reserva*, venerable and justly famous, which usually goes on sale after around 40 years! Not surprisingly it is very expensive and much sought after, and is made only in exceptional years. This outstanding wine is made from 70 per cent Tempranillo, 12 per cent Garnacha, 13 per cent Mazuelo and 5 per cent Graciano. There is also a distinctive old-style *reserva* rosé and a rounded, complex, 20-year-old, oaky white made from 95 per cent Viura and 5 per cent Malvasía. Another *reserva* white, **El Dorado de Murrieta**, contains 2 per cent Garnacha Blanca which replaces 2 per cent of the Viura, and there are also recent red and white wines labelled **Colección 2100**. Visits are by appointment on weekdays (mornings and afternoons, although 2 to 4pm should be avoided) for individuals and groups of no more than 18. An interpreter is available if required.

Marqués del Puerto (Fuenmayor, Alta, ☎ 941 450 001, ✉ 941 450 051) was founded in 1972 as **Bodegas López Agós**, but the name was changed to Marqués del Puerto in 1983 and is now part of the **Bebidas** group, along with **AGE** and **Campo Viejo**. This lovely bodega has an elegant spiral staircase leading down to the ageing cellars, which contain 4,200 barrels. They are a small firm producing carefully made wines in small quantities. The **Marqués del Puerto** label is used for the reds, which contain 85 per cent Tempranillo, Mazuelo and Graciano (although there is no Graciano in the *crianza*) up to *gran reserva*, and also the *joven* rosé and the barrel fermented 100 per cent Viura white. There is also a full range under the **Señorío de Agós** name. Group visits (no individuals) are by appointment (August closed). English and French are spoken.

Marqués de Riscal, Herederos del (Elciego, Alavesa, ☎ 941 606 000, ✉ 941 606 023) was founded in 1860 by Don Camilo, Hurtado de Amezaga, Marqués de Riscal, is the oldest bodega in Rioja and was the first to introduce the Bordeaux vinification system. It is a bodega built in cut stone in the typical style of the French Médoc châteaux, with 200ha (494 acres) of vineyards (Tempranillo, Graciano and Cabernet Sauvignon) and around 20,000 barrels. Marqués de Riscal produce light, dry, elegant wines comparing more with claret than Rioja, which age well and can be delicious. The bodega possesses a library of all vintages dating back to the very first. A little rosé is made from Tempranillo, while the new-style *Barón de Chirel*, with 50 per cent cabernet sauvignon, is outstanding and expensive. Individual and group visits are by appointment on weekdays from September to June (mornings only in July and closed in August). English and French are spoken.

Marqués de Vargas Bodegas y Viñedos (Logroño, Alta, ☎ 941 261 243) arrange visits by appointment on weekdays from 9.30am to 2pm, except during the harvest. English and French are spoken.

Marqués de Vitoria, Bodegas (Oyón, Alavesa, ☎/🖷 941 122 134) was founded in 1988. The bodega is of rustic construction with a wooden porch, although inside there are modern winemaking facilities and 1,300 barrels housed in a beautiful area with wooden ceilings and oak beams. It is one of only two bodegas (the other is *Viña Ijalba*) in Rioja making wine with ecologically grown grapes from their 170ha (420 acres) of vineyards. Visits are by appointment (individuals and groups) on weekday mornings and afternoons. There is a shop and French is spoken.

Martínez de Ayala, Bodegas (Labastida, Alavesa, ☎ 941 331 465) was founded in 1870 and is a small family bodega with traditional craftsmen, using not only the grapes from its own 10ha (25 acres) of vineyards, but also bought-in wine. They produce elegant, fresh reds that remain drinkable after 30 years or more, the oldest of which are labelled *Viña Mediate* or *Viña Meniguria*.

Martínez-Bujanda (Oyón, Alavesa, ☎ 941 122 188, 🖷 941 122 111) is a family run bodega established in 1889, situated in Oyón, a small village a few kilometres north of Logroño. A new bodega was opened in 1981 and the old one has been turned into a museum with tools and presses over 100 years old. They have 300ha (741 acres) of vineyards (spread over the Alavesa, Alta and Baja wine regions) and a well equipped bodega containing 12,500 barrels in a temperature and humidity controlled environment. Martínez-Bujanda produce distinctive, excellent wines in the modern fruity style, which are good value, including a fruity *sin crianza* red and a rosé.

The distinguished estate bottled **Conde de Valdemar** *crianza, reserva* and *gran reserva* use mainly Tempranillo with some Mazuelo from their vineyards in Oyón and Ausejo. They have had considerable success with an innovative 100 per cent Garnacha wine and are currently experimenting with Cabernet Sauvignon. The white Viura, which is fermented in wood on its lees for seven months, is a prestigious wine in Spain and fully justifies Jesus Martínez Bujanda's reputation as an excellent wine-maker. The **Martínez Bujanda** *reserva* is made with a special selection of their own grapes and is a spicy, fruity, full bodied red wine with a smooth finish.

A new winery in Fuenmayor began producing wine from the 1997 vintage. The red **Conde de Valdemar** red *crianza* (85 per cent Tempranillo and Mazuelo), undergoes a lengthy maceration to extract as much colour and flavour as possible from the skins without jeopardising the bouquet or complexity. It remains in the tanks for six months after which it is aged in American oak for a further 15 months – the resulting wine is full of flavour with a long finish and will keep for many years. A limited selection from the 1968 to 1978 vintages have been released. Martínez-Bujanda produce vintage wines only when the harvest meets the highest standards, and consequently, if you buy *Conde de Valdemar* wines you can be assured of consistent quality. Visits are on weekdays for individuals and groups. There is a museum and shop, and English, French and German are spoken.

Martínez Lacuesta (Haro, Alta, ☎ 941 310 050, 📠 941 303 748) was founded in 1895 by Felix Martínez and remains a family concern. The bodega consists of three stone buildings from the late 19th century, in addition to more modern ones, and contains 7,000 barrels together with their own cooper's workshop. The *reserva especial* is in the *gran reserva* class and is served at state banquets at the Spanish court. It ages well and a swirl of the glass releases all the complexity of its Tempranillo, Graciano and Mazuelo grapes and oak.

The *Campeador reserva* and *gran reserva*, sold in Burgundy style bottles, are produced only in good years and are quality, full-bodied, firm reds made from Garnacha and Tempranillo. The *Martínez Lacuesta* label is also used for a *reserva* and *crianza* red made from Tempranillo, Graciano and Mazuelo, a white *reserva* from Viura and Malvasía, plus a *joven* white and rosé. *Viña Delys* is a white *crianza* made from Viura and Malvasía. Individual and group visits are on weekday mornings from June to September and both mornings and afternoons from May to October (they are closed in August). French is spoken.

Mayor de Migueloa (Laguardia, Alavesa, ℃ 941 121 175, 🖷 941 121 022) was founded in 1987 and is housed in a baroque mansion built in 1619, complete with an underground cellar housing 100 barrels. The bodega has a hotel and restaurant, and daily visits are by appointment (individuals and groups) between 1 and 4pm and 9 and 11pm. There is a shop and English and French are spoken.

Mayorazgo Juan Zacarías de Bivián (Cuzcurrita, Alta, ℃ 941 301 626) can be visited by appointment on weekday mornings and afternoons (Saturdays – mornings only) from 9am to 2pm and 4 to 7pm. Tasting descriptions are given in French or Spanish.

Montecillo, Bodegas (Fuenmayor-Navarette, Alta, ℃ 941 440 125, 🖷 941 440 663) was founded in 1874 and is now owned by Osborne. A new bodega was built in 1974 and renovated in 1998-1999, and they also have a modern vinification plant near Navarette and a bodega with 13,700 barrels in Cenicero where wines are matured. Montecillo's old 100 per cent Tempranillo *gran reserva* under the *Viña Monty* label is a well balanced, complex, red. The names of *Viña Cumbrero* and *Montecillo* are also used. Individual and group visits on weekdays between 11am and 1pm (English and French are spoken).

Moreno Peña, David, *Provir* (Badarán, Alta ℃/🖷 941 367 338) was founded in 1981 and is situated 6km from the monasteries of Cañas and San Millán. They have a tiny 1ha (2.47 acres) vineyard and 700 barrels in an underground ageing cellar. Moreno Peña use bought-in grapes to produce good value red, white and rosé *jóvenes* using the *David Moreno*,

Monasterio de Yuso and *Orduña* labels, and in special years produce an excellent 100 per cent Tempranillo *Vallavares crianza*. Individual and group visits can be arranged on weekdays (mornings and afternoons) and Sundays (mornings only). English, French and Italian are spoken.

Muerza (San Adrián, Baja, ☎/✉ 948 670 054) was founded in 1882 and since 1986 has been owned by *Príncipe de Vianna* (Navarra DO). They have 25ha (62 acres) of vines and also use bought-in grapes and wine, and are now producing more mature wines from their 1,500 barrels. Those under the *Rioja Vega* label (with at least 85 per cent Tempranillo) are sound, fruity, woody, red *gran reservas*, *reservas* and *crianzas*, and there are also a *joven* red, white and rosé wines. The other label used, *Señorial*, also contains a complete range of wines.

Muga, Bodegas (Haro, Alta, ☎ 941 311 825, ✉ 941 312 867) was founded in 1932 and in 1971 moved to a new bodega near the railway station in Haro with 7,500 barrels (half American and half French). Around a third of the grapes are grown in their own 35ha (86 acres) vineyards, the remainder being bought-in from growers in Abalos. It is a small family run bodega making excellent, traditional Riojas which tend to be light, silky and aromatic, with a notable long, complex finish. The wines are still fermented in wooden vats and fined with egg whites. Muga are the only bodega in Rioja to use oak in all stages of vinification and ageing.

The *Prado Enea reservas* and *gran reservas* (80 per cent Tempranillo and 20 per cent Garnacha/Graciano) are powerful, distinctive velvety reds, sold in bottles with waxed capsules under the *Muga* label. There is also a barrel fermented white Viura and a good rosé made from Garnacha, Tempranillo and Viura. The modern generation of quality wine, *Torre Muga*, tastes delightfully different – it is produced from only the best vintages and matured in new barrels with optimum time in bottle. Muga also produce a 100 per cent Viura Cava, *Conde de Haro*. All the wines are made in traditional style by a small, dedicated workforce including the Muga brothers, and made with great care and pride. Weekday visits are by appointment (individuals and groups) from late June to September (between 9.30 and 11am) and from 22/9 and 20/6 from 9.30 to 11am and 4 to 6pm. There is an English-speaking guide in July only.

Muriel Bodegas (Elciego, Alavesa, ① 941 606 268, ✉ 941 606 371) was founded in 1934 and uses bought-in grapes and wines, which are aged in 4,000 barrels. Individual and group visits are by appointment on weekdays between 8.30am and 1.30pm and from 3.30 to 7.30pm.

Murúa, Bodegas (Elciego, Alavesa, ① 941 606 260, ✉ 941 606 326) was incorporated in 1964 and renovated in 1990, although the bodega itself is very old. It is surrounded by 110ha (272 acres) of vineyards and has 2,000 barrels. This small bodega produces *gran reserva* and *reserva Murúa* wines of finesse using 90 per cent Tempranillo, 8 per cent Graciano and 2 per cent of 'other' grapes. Visits for individuals and groups are by appointment on weekday mornings and afternoons, and include a library, which is of historical and oenological interest.

Murúa Entrena, Bodegas (Elciego, Alavesa, ① 941 106 268, ✉ 941 106 371) was founded in 1985 and produces *reserva* and *crianza* wines under two labels, *Viña Muriel* and *Julián Murúa Entrena*, plus red, white and rosé *jóvenes* labelled *El Somo*.

Navajas, Bodegas (Navarette, Alta, ① 941 440 140, ✉ 941 440 657) is a small producer with stainless steel fermentation tanks and well over 1,000 barrels, although it has only a small vineyard of 5ha (12 acres) and uses mainly bought-in grapes. The good value *Navajas* red *crianza* and *reserva* are full-bodied and fruity, and the range also includes an oak-aged white Viura. There is also a *joven* range using the *Navajas* label and a red *Corcuetos joven*. Also produced are reliable *crianza* and *joven* reds using the labels *Arjona, Crimol* and *Gustales* (*crianza* only). They all use the same 60 per cent Tempranillo, 20 per cent Garnacha and a 20 per cent blend of Mazuelo and Viura.

Olarra, Bodegas (Logroño, Alta, ① 941 235 299, ✉ 941 253 703) was founded in 1973 and is one of Rioja's showpieces, with a large, modern bodega situated on an industrial estate on the outskirts of Logroño. The bodega contains 17,500 barrels, 20 per cent in French oak, and all the grapes are bought-in. The modern building is unique and striking with a brick face, exposed concrete and Arabic tiles. It is has been dubbed the 'Cathedral of Rioja' and is built in the shape of a letter 'Y', its three 'wings' symbolising the three wine districts of Rioja.

Among Olarra's wines are the well-balanced, firm and silky **Cerro Anon** red *reserva* and *gran reserva*. The majority of wines are sold under the **Anares** label, including *joven* white and rosé, clean and fruity tasting, and *crianza*, *reserva* and *gran reserva* reds, each with progressively more wood and vanilla. There is also a *joven* Viura white, **Reciente**, and other *joven* wines under the label **Otoñal**, plus a *crianza* red. Individual and group visits are weekdays by appointment (English is spoken). There is a shop selling souvenirs and wine accessories.

Ondarre, Bodegas (Viana, Baja, ☎ 948 645 034, 📠 948 253 703) was founded in 1985 and is a modern striking building in stone with Arabic tiles. The bodega has 2,000 barrels for ageing. The **Ondarre** label is used for a wide range of wines from *jóvenes* to *gran reservas*, plus a Cava. A red *joven* is also produced under the **Viña Primera** label. Group visits are on weekdays by appointment and English is spoken.

Ontañón, Bodegas (Quel, Baja, ☎ 941 392 349, 📠 941 392 185 and also Logroño ☎/📠 941 234 200) was founded in 1985 by the Pérez Marco family, who, after supplying grapes to the big bodegas for many years, decided to form their own bodega. They have 70ha (173 acres) of vineyards. Ontañón's reliable wines are labelled **Artesa** and include particularly well rounded, complex, well-made *reservas* and *gran reservas*. **Comportillo**, is a fruity red *crianza* and **Señorío de Villoslada** and **Fidencio** are *joven* reds with 70 per cent Tempranillo and 30 per cent Garnacha.

Ontañón *reserva* is a limited production red made with 95 per cent Tempranillo and 5 per cent Graciano, the latter from their La Montesa vineyard, which has an exceptional micro-climate. Aged in both American and French oak barrels, the wines are racked every three or four months and fined with egg whites every four months. This elegant wine, with its attractive deep red colour, rich, mature fruit taste is complemented by cigar box and dark chocolate overtones, and should last for many years.

The new bodega, situated ten minutes from the centre of Logroño on the N232 road (km3) to Zaragossa, contains exquisite paintings, sculptures and stained-glass windows commissioned from a local artist, and a museum is also planned. No appointments are necessary for visits from Mondays to Saturdays between 11am and 1pm and 5 to 7pm. Visits (English spoken) to the Quel bodega are arranged on weekday mornings and afternoons by appointment (individuals and groups) and you can also visit their museum containing paintings and statues. There is an interesting church nearby. Both bodegas are well worth a visit. English is spoken.

Ostatu, Bodegas (Samaniego, Alavesa, ☎ 941 609 133, ✉ 941 609 104), founded in 1720, is housed in a neo-classical stone palace and started life as an inn. An extension added to the old mansion (which is an architectural landmark and a protected building) was sympathetically designed to compliment the original building down to the smallest detail. Ostatu have 25ha (62 acres) of vineyards and 250 barrels. Individual and group visits are daily by appointment from 9am until 2pm.

Palacio, Bodegas (Laguardia, Alavesa, ☎ 941 600 057, ✉ 941 600 297) is an old family firm founded in 1894 which parted company with Seagram's in 1987, since when it has regained its former reputation. The bodega contains 5,150 barrels of American and French oak, although new barrels are French and will eventually replace the American. In 1991, a fruity and floral red, 100 per cent Tempranillo joven, *Milflores*, was introduced in a fancy millefiore bottle. *Glorioso crianza, reserva* and *gran reserva*, are typical, reliable 100 per cent Tempranillo reds aged in French oak. The *Cosme Palacio y Hermanos* label includes a reliable red *crianza*, soft, red fruit flavour with vanilla overtones, plus a *joven* white. The fruity red *joven El Portico* completes an excellent range of wines. Visits by individuals (group visits are by appointment only) are organised on the hour from 11am to 2pm, Tuesdays to Fridays, and from noon to 2pm on Saturdays and Sundays. There is also a shop.

Palacios Remondo, Bodegas (Alfaro, Baja, ☎ 941 237 177, ✉ 941 247 798) was founded in 1947 in Alfaro, although wines have also been made near Haro since 1990, where the founder's son, Antonio, has created a château-like estate. The Head office is in Logroño. They have 150ha (371 acres) of vineyards and 2,000 barrels, around one-fifth in French oak.

The better wines are sold under the ***Herencia Remondo*** label and the reds up to *gran reserva*, when at their best, are elegant and complex with a hint of wood. ***Plácet*** is a creamy rounded, buttery white, which is fermented in temperature-controlled, 15,000-litre, new French-oak barrels. Their white and rosé *jóvenes* are well made and labelled ***José Palacios*** after the founder. Other labels used are ***Capa Remondo*** and ***Distinción***. Individual and group visits are daily from 9am to 1pm and 4 to 7pm, including a wine museum containing old vinification tools. English and French are spoken. The bodega also has its own well-equipped hotel with 85 rooms, four restaurants (excellent food) and a swimming pool.

Palacio Sáez, Luis María (Elciego, Alavesa, ☎ 941 606 305, 🖷 941 606 172) was founded in 1968 by the heirs of the Marquis of Legarda. The bodega has 17ha (42 acres) of vineyards and three cellars (with cut-stone arches dating back at least 400 years) containing 200 barrels. Their wines are labelled *Palacio Sáez* and *Hacienda Palaciana*, the latter including a red *crianza* (90 per cent Tempranillo, 5 per cent each of Graciano and Viura) and a *reserva* (95 per cent Tempranillo and 5 per cent Graciano) produced only in limited quantities. Visits by individuals and groups are daily (all day) except Sundays, when they are afternoons only. French is spoken.

Pascual Larrieta, Miguel Angel (Samaniego, Alavesa, ☎ 941 609 059, 🖷 941 415 872) was founded in 1790 and is a modern bodega with an 18th century underground vaulted cellar with an antique two-screw manual press on display. They have 12ha (30 acres) of vineyards and produce a *joven* red Tempranillo, ***Pascual Larrieta***, by carbonic maceration. Individual and group visits by appointment, mornings (8am to 1pm) and afternoons (4 to 8pm).

Paternina, Federico, Bodegas (Haro, Alta, ☎ 941 310 550, 🖷 941 312 778), owned by Don Marcos Eguizabel, was founded in 1898 in Ollauri, although it has since moved its production to a large modern bodega on the outskirts of Haro. However, Paternina still store many superb, rare old vintages in their original deep cellars at Ollauri, which were dug during the 16th century by Portuguese workers. These blackened, musty cellars with low corridors and dripping walls, although a bit spooky, are well worth seeing.

Paternina's best-known **Banda** range includes a light red *crianza*, **Banda Azul** (75 per cent Tempranillo, 25 per cent Garnacha), a *joven* white, **Banda Dorada** (100 per cent Viura), best drunk young, and a *joven* rosé, **Banda Rosa** (60 per cent Tempranillo, 20 per cent Garnacha and 20 per cent Viura). The **Federico Paternina** *gran reserva* (70 per cent Tempranillo, 20 per cent Garnacha and 10 per cent Mazuelo) has more personality, with lots of wood and vanilla, and is aged in the cellars at Ollauri. The superb **Conde de los Andes** (95 per cent Tempranillo and 5 per cent Mazuelo) is made only in excellent years and is also aged at Ollauri. The **Viña Vial** *reserva,* made with the same grape proportions as the Federico Paternina *gran reserva*, is another smooth, mature red. The white **Rinsol** is made from the first pressing of Viura grapes and is a light, elegant, fruity white wine, while the *joven* **Monte Haro** white is 90 per cent Viura and 10 per cent Garnacha Blanca. Visits (individuals and groups) by appointment daily (except Sundays), mornings and afternoons.

Pedro Martínez Alesanco, Bodegas, *Provir* (Badarán, Alta, ℰ 941 367 075) have 30ha (74 acres) of vineyards producing good quality, aromatic *joven* wines (sold under their own label) made using carbonic maceration. The red *joven* contains 70 per cent Tempranillo, 25 per cent Garnacha and a 5 per cent blend of Graciano, Viura and Malvasía, while the white is 100 per cent Viura and the rosé 80 per cent Garnacha and 20 per cent Viura. All grapes are grown in their own vineyard, the white grapes from vines over 25 years old. No appointment is necessary for daily visits.

Pérez Artacho, Manuel (Cenicero, Alta, ☎ 941 454 204) was founded in 1982. They have 20ha (49 acres) of vineyards and use traditional vinification from their own harvest. Their *joven Pérez Artacho* red and rosé wines contain 80 per cent Tempranillo, 15 per cent Viura and 5 per cent Mazuelo. No appointment is necessary for daily visits between 9am and 8pm.

Pérez Foncea Bodegas, *Provir* (Fuenmayor, Alta ☎   941 450 142) have 30ha (74 acres) of vineyards and over 600 barrels. The *Señorío de la Luz* label is used for *joven* red, white and rosé – the latter two are excellent with seafood – while the *Vallemayor* label is used for the excellent red *reserva* and *gran reserva*. The modern-style, semi-*crianza* **Tondeluna** red is selected as the red house wine of many prestigious restaurants and the production of all their wines is quality orientated.

Pérez Maestresala, Alberto (Villabuena, Alavesa, ☎ 941 609 076) was founded in 1985 and is a modern bodega with old-style vaulted cellars and 16.5ha (41 acres) of vineyards. They use two labels, *José María y Primitivo Pérez* for their red *joven* and **Maestresala** for their older red. Individual and group visits are daily by appointment.

Perica Bodegas (San Asensio, Alta, ☎ 941 417 152. ▨ 941 457 240) was founded in 1991 in an old building with a small cellar cut from solid rock and has 37ha (91 acres) of vineyards and 1,100 barrels. Perica produces quality wines, the best of which include the *crianza* and *reserva* reds using the *Viña Olagosa* label, although the *Perica gran reserva* (made with all four of Rioja's official red grape varieties) is their most prestigious wine. *Joven* red, white and rosé are also sold under the *Perica* and *Mi Villa* labels, containing different proportions of the same grapes. Individual and group visits are by appointment on weekday mornings from 10am to 1pm.

Primicia (Laguardia, Alavesa, ☎ 941 600 296, ▨ 945 145 029) was founded in 1985 and is a small, quality bodega with 25ha (62 acres) of vineyards, 1,100 French Limousin barrels as well as stainless steel tanks. The best reds (100 per cent Tempranillo) use the *Viña Diezmo* label for the *crianzas* and *reservas*, while the rosé is 75 per cent Tempranillo and 25 per cent Viura. They also use the *Besagain* label for a range of *joven* red, white and rosé, together with a red 100 per cent Tempranillo *crianza*. Visits are by appointment.

Propiedad Grial (Fuenmayor, Alta, ☎ 941 450 194) was founded in 1982 and is a small modern bodega surrounded by its own 20ha (49 acres) of vineyards and it owns 510 barrels. Grial produce *Gribeña*, a red *crianza* made from 85 per cent Tempranillo, 10 per cent Mazuelo and 5 per cent Viura. Daily visits are by appointment for individuals and groups. English is spoken.

Puelles Fernández, Jesús y Félix, *Provir* (Abalos, Alta, ☎ 941 334 415, ✉ 941 334 132) is a new stone construction built around a 17th century family mill (*molino*), originally the town hall, situated on the outskirts of Abalos in a beautiful natural setting on the slopes of the Sierra de Cantabria mountain rage. The bodega has 10ha (25 acres) of vineyards and 510 barrels (80 per cent American oak and 20 per cent French). Puelles operate a wine club, *Club del Molino,* whose members can have their wines individually labelled. Tempranillo, Graciano, Mazuelo and Viura are all used in their fine *crianza*, *reserva* and *gran reserva* reds, and they also make a popular fruity, un-oaked *cosecheros* red and a fruity white Viura. The wines are all labelled *Puelles*. Visits are by appointment daily (English spoken) and if you arrive at 4.30pm you will be given a full one-hour tour of the bodega plus the fascinating water mill.

Quintana Quintana, Ponciano (Labastida, Alavesa, ☎ 941 331 022) was founded in 1950 and has 7.3ha (18 acres) of vineyards and 100 barrels stored in 250-year-old cellars with vaulted ceilings hewn out of solid rock. They produce *joven* red and *reserva* wines made from their own Tempranillo and Garnacha grapes using the *Matzalde* label. Individual and group visits are on weekdays by appointment.

Ramírez, Bodegas, *Provir* (San Vicente de la Sonsierra, Alta ☎ 941 334 074, ✉ 944 261 102) was founded in 1987, but although the bodega is recently constructed the original bodega (built 60 years ago) is still in existence. The bodega has 8ha (20 acres) of excellently situated vineyards and 350 barrels, and combines traditional skills with modern technology using carbonic maceration. The *Ramírez de la Piscina* label is used for their quality *joven*, *crianza* and *reserva* reds made from 90 per cent Tempranillo and 10 per cent Viura. They also make a *joven* white and rosé. Individual and group visits by appointment (French is spoken).

Ramón Bilbao, Bodegas (Haro, Alta, ① 941 310 295, 🖷 941 310 835) was founded in 1924, with a new bodega built in 1972 in typical Riojan style. They have around 10ha (25 acres) of vineyards and 4,500 barrels, with most wines being bought-in. Ramón Bilbao produce quality wines, the best of which is the Tempranillo *Viña Turzaballa gran reserva*, which is given plenty of time in American oak and bottle. Other wines under the *Ramón Bilbao* label include white, red and rosé *jóvenes*, a *crianza* (80 per cent Tempranillo, 15 per cent Garnacha and 5 per cent Mazuelo), a *reserva* (80 to 85 per cent Tempranillo, 15 to 20 per cent Garnacha and 5 per cent Mazuelo) and a *gran reserva* (90 per cent Tempranillo and a 10 per cent blend of Garnacha, Mazuelo and Graciano). Group visits are by appointment on weekday mornings and afternoons.

Real Compañía de Vinos (Cenicero, Alta, ① 941 454 007, 🖷 941 454 530) was founded in 1949 and has 5ha (12 acres) of vineyards and 1,500 barrels. The original old stone and wood building was constructed in the mid-1800s and owned by Benedictine monks who distilled liqueurs there until as recently as 1949, when it was then converted to a bodega (restored in 1988). They produce quality red *crianza* and *reserva* wines under the *Marqués de San Román* label, using 80 per cent Tempranillo, 15 per cent Graciano and Garnacha, plus 5 per cent Mazuelo for the *crianza* and a small percentage of Viura for the *reserva*. *Barón de Lardies* is a *joven* range containing the same grape varieties (as above) in slightly different proportions. Visits by appointment daily (except Sundays) from 9am to 5pm.

Real Divisa (Abalos, Alta, ① 941 334 118, 🖷 941 218 155) make worthy reds, mainly using Tempranillo, labelled as *Marqués de Legarda*. See *Bodegas de la Real Divisa*.

Reja Dorada Bodegas (Logroño, Alta, ① 942 236 980) are situated in the old part of Logroño and are the oldest bodega in the town. They have 500 barrels and use the *Revellín* label for their *crianza* red, white and rosé wines, and *Vigenza* for their *joven* range. Weekday visits by appointment.

Remélluri, La Granja (Labastida, Alavesa, *Granja Nuestra Señora de Remélluri*, ① 941 331 274, 🖷 941 331 441) was founded in 1967 and is situated at the foot of the Sierra de Cantabria mountain range. The main building was constructed in the 18th century and the farm (*granja*) was originally owned by the Monastery of Toloño and home to 300 monks. There is an 11th to 12th century necropolis (burial site) on the estate, a 13th century shrine and a museum. The owners, Señor Salis and his family, have invested considerable time and money in restoring the *granja*, replanted the 65ha (160 acres) vineyard, and installed modern stainless steel tanks to supplement the large oak vats and 3,500 barrels.

Remélluri describe themselves as 'new traditionalists' and are a small estate making good, consistently high quality wines under the guidance of Telmo Rodríguez, their dynamic young winemaker. Their single-vineyard, red *reserva* and *gran reserva* **Remélluri** (both 100 per cent Tempranillo) are of consistently high quality, and even in average years they produce good wines (in excellent years they are outstanding). Individual and group visits are Mondays to Saturdays between 8am and noon, and 3 to 5pm. English and French are spoken.

Remírez de Ganuza (Samaniego, Alavesa) make strong (up to 14 per cent alcohol), well-made, estate-bottled wines, smooth and full-bodied, and produced from old vines. The 1992 *reserva* is 90 per cent Tempranillo and 10 per cent Graciano. They are expensive.

Río Estébas, César del, Bodegas, *Provir* (Cordovin, Alta ① 941 367 061) was founded in 1982 and is a typical Rioja bodega with a deep cellar, cut stone stairs and a vaulted barrel-ageing area. The fruity, polished *César del Río jóvenes* are carefully produced by carbonic maceration using 75 per cent Garnacha Tinta and 25 per cent Viura, and are ideal served chilled as an aperitif. Individual and group visits by appointment on weekdays (mornings and afternoons).

Rioja Santiago (Haro, Alta, ① 941 310 200, ▤ 941 312 679) was founded in 1870 in Labastida, making it the third-oldest bodega in Rioja. They have no vineyards and no vinification as they use bought-in wine, which is aged in 1,227 barrels. The older *Gran Condal* and *Gran Enológica* labels are their best reds, which are produced only in excellent years, using 85 per cent Tempranillo and 15 per cent Garnacha. The *Vizconde de Ayala, Rioja Santiago, Puente de Haro, Castillo de Ezpeleta* and *Bilibio* labels also use the same grapes for their *crianza, reserva* and *gran reserva* wines. All these labels include *joven* red, white and rosé, the whites being 100 per cent Viura and the rosés 70 per cent Tempranillo and 30 per cent Viura. Visits by individuals and groups are by appointment on weekday mornings from 9am to 2pm. English is spoken.

Riojanas, Bodegas (Cenicero, Alta, ☎ 941 454 050, ⊟ 941 454 529) was founded in 1890. The old bodega is a 19th century reproduction of a Bordeaux château, complete with Gothic windows and crenellations, while the gates to the vineyard date back to 1799. The bodega, which had a number of additions between 1940 and 1990, has 200ha (494 acres) of vineyards and 20,000 barrels. Bodegas Riojanas produce quality wines including the traditional, elegant, oaky red *Viña Albina reserva* and *gran reserva* (80 per cent Tempranillo, 15 per cent Mazuelo and 5 per cent Graciano). The dark, plummy *Monte Real reserva* and *gran reserva* are made from the same grapes as Viña Albina, but has more colour and alcohol, and a vanilla spice finish.

The white *Monte Real crianza* is an interesting wine, with 30 per cent Tempranillo, 30 per cent Garnacha and 40 per cent Viura, and there is also a fairly full-bodied rosé. The young *joven* red, white and rosé are labelled *Canchales*. There is also the *Puerta Vieja* range of red *crianza* (same grape blend as Monte Real), a 95 per cent Viura and 5 per cent Malvasía *joven* white, and a 30 per cent Tempranillo, 30 per cent Garnacha and 40 per cent Viura rosé. All Bodegas Riojanas' wines have a good reputation and are constantly improving in quality. Weekday visits by individuals are at 11am (groups by appointment only). There is a shop and English, French and German are spoken.

Roda, Bodegas (Haro, Alta, ☎ 941 303 001, ⊟ 941 312 703) produce superb, smooth, modern-style, fruity, elegant estate-bottled reds. *Roda 1* and *Roda 11* use slightly different proportions of Tempranillo and Garnacha, for example, the splendid 1994 Roda 1 *reserva* has 83 per cent Tempranillo and 17 per cent Garnacha, while the 1995 Roda II *reserva* uses 77 per cent Tempranillo and 23 per cent Garnacha. The vines used are at least 30 years old and the wines are aged in French oak barrels. Visits are by appointment (English and French are spoken).

Rubí, Bodegas (Haro, Alta, ① 941 310 937, ▭ 941 311 602) was founded in 1989 and is a modern concrete and stone structure with vaulted cellars. Rubí own just 2ha (5 acres) of vineyards and have 1,200 barrels. They produce an excellent range of wines under the *Viña Olabarri* label which include a *crianza* (100 per cent Tempranillo), a *reserva* (90 per cent Tempranillo and a 10 per cent blend of Mazuelo and Garnacha Tinta) and a *gran reserva* with 80 per cent Tempranillo and a 20 per cent blend of Mazuelo and Garnacha. *Solar Teules* is the label for their range of *jóvenes*. Visits are by appointment on weekday mornings and afternoons, except for June to September, when they are mornings only.

Salazar Rodrigo, Julián (Villabueno, Alavesa, ① 941 609 066) was founded in 1905 and is an old bodega hewn from the solid rock, known locally as the 'bodega of the priests' as it was originally used to store religious artefacts. Its *Viña Salazar* is an aromatic, fruity *joven* red made with Tempranillo and Viura. The bodega has 15ha (37 acres) of vineyards. Visits daily by appointment.

Salceda, Viña (Elciego, Alavesa, ① 941 606 125, ▭ 941 142 347) is a medium-size bodega of modern construction founded in 1969, with stainless steel fermentation tanks dating from 1974 and 7,000 barrels. Its well balanced *Viña Salceda* red *crianza* contains 90 per cent Tempranillo, while the *Conde de la Salceda reservas* and *gran reservas* (containing 95 per cent Tempranillo) are rich quality reds. Individual and group visits by appointment are on weekdays – mornings from 9am to 1pm and afternoons from 3.30 to 6pm. English is spoken.

San Gregorio, S. Coop Bodegas (Azagra, Baja, ①/▭ 941 692 137) was founded in 1950 and has a vast 900ha (2,223 acres) of vineyards. *Viña Zagra, Orobon* and *Argadile* labels are used for their *joven* reds and rosés containing Tempranillo and Garnacha. Visits are by appointment on Tuesdays and Thursdays (mornings and afternoons).

San Isidro, Coop, Bodegas (Calahorra, Baja, ①/▭ 941 130 626) was founded in 1959 and is of new construction with 160ha (395 acres) of vineyards. They produce a range of *joven* wines under four labels: *Dunviro, Monte Padillares, Nasica* and *Lozoniel*. Visits are by appointment daily (mornings and afternoons) except Sundays.

San Justo y San Isidro S Coop (Quel, Baja, ②/✉ 941 392 030) was founded in 1947. They produce a Tempranillo and Garnacha *joven* red, a Viura white and Garnacha rosé under the *Fuenta Yedra* label, plus a *joven* Garnacha rosé with the *Marcuera* label. Visits are by appointment Mondays to Wednesdays and Fridays from 8am to 1pm and 3 to 6pm.

San Miguel S Coop, Bodegas (Ausejo, Baja, ② 941 430 005, ✉ 941 430 209) was founded in 1956 and has 550ha (1,359 acres) of vineyards and ageing facilities containing 225 barrels. Their wines include *Peña Vieja*, a red *crianza* made from 75 per cent Tempranillo, 15 per cent Garnacha and a 10 per cent blend of Mazuelo and Garnacha. They also produce a range of *joven* wines under the *Compolosa* label, which include a red with the same blend of grapes as the Peña Vieja *crianza*, a 100 per cent Viura white and a 100 per cent Garnacha rosé. San Miguel also use the *Viña Antiqua* label. Visits are by appointment.

San Roque Cooperativa (Alcanadre, Baja, ② 941 604 005) was founded in 1957 and is one of the best co-ops in Rioja with access to 600ha (1,493 acres) of vineyards. They use the *Aradón* label for their 100 per cent Viura white and *joven* red (70 per cent Tempranillo, 25 per cent Garnacha and 5 per cent Viura), both of which are consistently good and sometimes excellent. The rosé *joven* is 50 per cent Garnacha and Viura.

San Sixto, Coop, Bodegas (Yecora, Alavesa, ② 941 601 448) was founded in 1953 and has 200ha (494 acres) of vineyards. Daily visits are by appointment, including sightseeing tours of Yecora to view the 12th century fountain, 13th century shrine and 16th century church.

Santa Daría, Coop, Bodegas (Cenicero, Alta, ② 941 454 110, ✉ 941 454 618) was founded in 1963 with a concrete basement containing 2,300 barrels of French and American oak. They have a massive 900ha (2,223 acres) of vineyards and new stainless steel vinification facilities. The *Santa Daría* label is used for a range of *crianza* and *reserva* reds in addition to red, white and rosé *joven* wines. Santa Daría also use the *Valdemontán* label for a similar range of 100 per cent Tempranillo reds and 100 per cent Viura whites. Visits are by appointment on weekday mornings and afternoons (French is spoken).

Santamaría, Güénaga, Eusebio (Laguardia, Alavesa, ☏ 941 600 110) was founded in 1300 and the bodega originally belonged to Samaniego, a Spanish writer of fables. They produce *Decidido*, a fruity, *joven* Tempranillo red. Group and individual visits by appointment.

Santamaría López (Laguardia, Alavesa, ☏ 941 121 212, ☎ 941 121 222) was founded in 1937, and totally renovated in 1994 and has an impressive cellar containing 1,500 barrels of American and French oak, They produce a quality range of wines using an assortment of labels. Tempranillo, Garnacha, Graciano and Mazuelo are used in the reds produced under the labels of *Solar Gran*, *Viña Huerco reserva* and *Solar Viejo*, while *Viña Mantibre* includes *jóvenes* as well as a red *reserva* and *crianza*. *Viña Gloria* and *Laguardia Real* are both red *crianzas*, while *Arbulo* and *Ordate* are both red *jóvenes*. All use the four official red grape varieties and the whites are 100 per cent Viura. Visits are by appointment for individuals and groups on weekday mornings during the summer, and mornings and afternoons in winter. English and French are spoken.

Santuario Vinícola Riojano (Arnedillo, Baja, ☏ 941 394 063, ☎ 941 383 860) was founded in 1980 and is built around a 300-year-old mill. The château-style bodega is situated on the banks of the Cidacos River surrounded by mountains and just one kilometre from the well-known Arnedillo health spa. The bodega has a tiny 1.6ha (4 acres) vineyard and 103 barrels. They produce red *crianzas* and *reservas* using the labels *Viña Ritual* and *Ritual*, the latter containing 10 per cent Mazuelo rather than Viura with 75 per cent Tempranillo and Garnacha. The *Pedro Garrida* label is used for the *joven* range. Individual and group visits daily between 10am and 8pm. English and Japanese are spoken.

"A fount of wisdom, merriment and contentment; wine speaks."

Anon

Señorío de Arana (Labastida, Alavesa, ☎ 941 331 150) was founded in 1980 and has 5ha (12 acres) of vineyards and 1,200 barrels. They use the *Viña del Oja* label for a red *reserva*, consisting of Tempranillo, Mazuelo and Graciano. The *crianza* is made from Tempranillo, Garnacha and Mazuelo, and the red *joven* from Tempranillo, Garnacha and Viura. There is also a white and a rosé in the range. Visits by individuals and groups are by appointment on weekday mornings and afternoons.

Señorío de Líbano, Bodegas (Sajazarra, Alta, ☎ 941 320 066, ☎ 941 320 251) was founded in 1973 in a 15th century medieval castle and has 22ha (54 acres) of vineyards and 1,500 barrels. They produce good quality aged wines including *Castillo de Sajazarra reserva*, which contains up to 25 per cent Garnacha, plus Tempranillo and Viura. The label *Sénorío Líbano* is used for another red *reserva*. Individual and group visits are by appointment on weekday mornings and afternoons. English and French are spoken.

Señorío de San Vicente (San Vicente de la Sonsierra, Alta, ☎ 941 308 040, ☎ 941 334 371) was founded in 1991 and is housed in a 150-year-old building, which has been fully restored complete with two new ageing areas containing 800 barrels. It also has a hall with 15,000-litre wooden vats, a six metre high ageing chamber with a stone vault and a bottle ageing area with a wooden roof. The bodega has 18ha (44 acres) of vineyards. Daily visits by appointment (individuals and groups) mornings and afternoons except Sundays. English and French are spoken.

Señorío de Villarica, *Provir* (San Asensio, Alta, ☎ 941 457 171, ☎ 941 457 172) was founded in 1984 and has modern stainless steel tanks. It uses all four of Rioja's official red grape varieties and carbonic maceration for the reliable *Cantalosgallos jóvenes*. The good quality *crianzas*, *reservas* and *gran reservas* (as well as the well-known *Clarete de San Asensio*) are labelled *Señorío de Villarrica*, while there is also a *reserva* and *gran reserva* under the *Delicia de Baco* label.

Sierra Cantabria, Bodegas, *Provir* (San Vicente de la Sonsierra, Alta, ☎ 941 334 080, ☎ 941 334 371) was founded in 1954 (it was originally *Bodegas Eguren*) and is built in contemporary style using 300-year-old cut stone. They have 85ha (210 acres) of vineyards and around 1,000 barrels. Sierra

Cantabria are one of the leaders in young wines made by carbonic maceration with great skill. Their *Murmurón* (85 per cent Tempranillo and 15 per cent Viura) is a fruity red with plenty of body – in fact all their wines have more colour and strength than the average Rioja Alavesa wine. The *Sierra Cantabria crianza, reserva* and *gran reserva* are well balanced and full of taste, containing Tempranillo and Garnacha, plus 5 per cent Viura added to the *crianza*. Other labels include *Bodega Eguren* and *Códice*, which are easy drinking with a taste of cherries. Individual and group visits are weekdays (mornings and afternoons) by appointment. French is spoken.

SMS, Bodegas (Villabueno, Alavesa, ☎ 941 609 085, ▭ 941 123 304) was founded in the late 1800s and originally called *Marqués de la Solana*. SMS are the initials of the three families, Samaniego, Miláns del Bosch and Solana who own this small family concern. They have 50ha (124 acres) of vineyards and 900 barrels, and all their quality red wines are produced in limited quantities as single-estate wines. Up to the early '80s the grapes were not de-stalked and the older wines are darker in colour and slower maturing than most from Alavesa. The later wines are fragrant (with a touch of cedar), full-bodied and fruity with a long finish.

The SMS brand name is *Valserrano*, containing Tempranillo with a little Graciano and Mazuelo, and aged in American oak barrels to give a touch of vanilla to these rich, fruity, complex wines. The excellent white, made from 100 per cent Viura grapes picked from the sunniest areas at the height of their ripeness, has a complex fruitiness influenced by six months in French Allier and Vosges oak barrels. SMS also produce an interesting deep coloured red made from 100 per cent Graciano, with an intense fruity aroma. Visits (individuals and groups) are by appointment on weekday mornings and afternoons.

Solábal Bodegas y Viñedos (Abalos, Alta, ☎ 941 334 492) was founded in 1988 and has 75ha (185 acres) of vineyards and 160 barrels. They use the labels *Solabal* (red *crianza* and *joven* rosé) and *Muñarrate* (a red *joven* made by carbonic maceration), and are of sound quality produced mainly from Tempranillo and 20 per cent Viura. Individual and group visits by appointment, mornings and afternoons.

Solana de Ramírez Ruíz Bodegas (Abalos, Alta, ☎/✉ 941 308 049) was founded in 1985. The bodega is situated in the old centre of Abalos and is a modern building designed in the form of a castle, and blends perfectly with the surrounding old houses and trees. Solana de Ramírez have 35ha (86 acres) of vineyards, 286 barrels and modern stainless steel facilities complemented by old wooden vats. Daily visits by appointment for individuals and groups.

Sonsierra, S. Coop, Bodegas (San Vicente de la Sonsierra, Alta, ☎ 941 334 031, ✉ 941 334 245) was founded in 1961 and the winemaking facilities expanded in 1989, while new bottling and ageing facilities were added in 1994. The Co-op has almost 250 members with 600ha (1,482 acres) of vineyards and 1,250 barrels. They produce red, white and rosé *jóvenes* under the *Sonsierra* label, together with a red *crianza* (100 per cent Tempranillo), and *Viña Mindiarte* red *crianza* and *reserva* (also 100 per cent Tempranillo), which are of higher quality. Visits are by appointment (English spoken).

Telmo Rodríguez, **one of the modern young Bordeaux trained winemakers at Bodegas Remelurri in Labastida, applies modern techniques to the grapes of old bush vines, producing excellent wines.**

Torre de Oña, Bodegas (Laguardia/Páganos, Alavesa, ☎ 941 121 154, ✉ 941 127 111) was founded in 1987 but has since been sold to *Bodegas La Rioja Alta*, who sensibly have allowed it to continue making modern style Rioja. It is situated at the foot of the Sierra de Cantabria mountains between Laguardia and Páganos on the old pilgrim route to Compostela, and is a traditional Alavesa-style building in cut stone containing stainless steel tanks. They have 50ha (123 acres) of Rioja's choicest vineyards, containing Tempranillo, Mazuelo and some Cabernet Sauvignon for experimental purposes (the 1994 reserva contains 4 per cent Cabernet Sauvignon). The aim is to produce excellent *reservas* and these splendid, single vineyard estate wines are certainly worth seeking out.

The vines are trained, *en espaldera*, which exposes the grapes to greater light, allowing better ripening conditions and cleaner, healthier grapes. The yield is stringently controlled to obtain optimum quality fruit, and fermentation takes place in stainless steel tanks under controlled conditions. The 4,000 maturation barrels are mostly new French and American oak, and the wine spends two years ageing before being fined with egg white, followed by bottling and a further two years maturation. The outstanding, intense, deep red **Barón de Oña** (mainly Tempranillo with a little Mazuelo) has a ripe fruit bouquet and a well-balanced intense taste and long finish. It is a good example of the new-style Riojas – deep-red, fruity but with less oak overtones. Visits are by appointment (individuals and groups) mornings and afternoons except Sundays. French is spoken.

Torres – Librada, Hnos, *Provir* (Alfaro, Baja ① 941 180 249, ⌨ 941 182 200,) was founded in 1987. The bodega is surrounded by 20ha (49 acres) of vineyards in Estarijo, with the bodega installations housed in the remains of an old military airfield with 183 barrels of French and American oak. Torres produce well made reds using the label **Torrescudo** for their *crianza* and *reserva*, containing 90 per cent Tempranillo and a 10 per cent blend of Mazuelo and Graciano, while the **Estarijo** label is used for their 100 per cent Tempranillo red *joven*. Weekday visits by appointment (French is spoken).

Unión de Cosecheros de Labastida (Labastida, Alavesa, ①/⌨ 941 331 161) is one of the highest quality co-ops in Rioja with around 160 members and many renowned names among their clients. They have 450ha (1,111 acres) of vineyards, and 2,000 barrels. Some of their wines are sold under the label **Montebuena**, including white and rosé *jóvenes* and a 100 per cent Tempranillo red *crianza*. **Solagüen** is used for a reliable range of 100 per cent Tempranillo red *crianza*, *reserva* and *gran reserva* wines. **Manuel Quintana, Castillo, Labastida** *gran reserva* and **Gastrijo** *reserva* labels have also been used. Visits by individuals and groups are by appointment.

Unión de Viticultores Riojanas (Fuenmayor, Alta, ① 941 451 129, ⌨ 941 450 297, ✉ uvrioja@apdo.com) was founded in 1996 and is housed in an elegant cut-stone building containing 2,200 barrels. Only a limited number of vintages are produced. Individual and group visits are daily (mornings and afternoons) by appointment. English, French and German are spoken.

Urarte Espinosa, Juan José (Assa, Alavesa, ☎ 941 600 102) was founded in 1290 and this very old bodega was associated with Don Juan, *El Bravo,* King of Navarra. The bodega includes paddocks, a 1,000-year-old oak tree, and a cave dating from 1250, which was excavated in 1286 and now contains 150 barrels. The *Viña Emilliano* label is used for a red *joven* and *crianza*, both made from 70 per cent Tempranillo, 15 per cent Viura, 10 per cent Mazuelo and 5 per cent other varieties. Individual and group visits daily by appointment. The bodega has dining facilities and bullfights are an added attraction (for some!). There are also scenic walks by the river and local tours can be arranged.

Urbina Benito, Pedro (Cuzcurrita de Río Trinon, Alta, ☎/🖷 941 224 272) was founded in the 19th century and has 50ha (123 acres) of vineyards and 640 barrels. The bodega has cut-stone cellars containing old oak vats, an old vinification building and a newer structure in concrete. *Urbina* is an excellent, high quality wine of limited production and the *Urbina reserva especial* is produced only in excellent years, such as 1994. The *crianza*, *reserva* and *gran reserva* reds are mainly Tempranillo plus Graciano and Mazuelo, and there is also a 100 per cent Viura *joven* white and a *joven* rosé of Garnacha and Viura. Visits are by appointment for individuals and groups. English and French are spoken.

Valdelana, Juan Jesús (Elciego, Alavesa, ☎ 941 606 055, 🖷 941 606 011) was founded in 1877, with the cellars and façade in cut stone built around the same time. They have 25ha (62 acres) of vineyards and 300 barrels, and the grapes are still crushed by foot in the old fashioned way. The *Valdelana* label is used for a red *crianza* and red, white and rosé *jóvenes*, while *Juan Valdelana* is a red *joven*. Visits by individuals and groups are on weekdays by appointment between 8am and 9pm, weekends 8am to 3pm. There is a small museum and English and French are spoken.

Valgrande, Bodegas (San Vicente de la Sonsierra, Alta, ☎/🖷 947 545 609) was founded in 1970 and has 500 barrels.

No appointments are necessary for visits at any time (but check on festival dates) and both English and French are spoken.

Vallemayor, Bodegas (Fuenmayor, Alta, ☎ 941 450 142, 🖷 941 450 376) was founded in 1985 with 25ha (62 acres) of vineyards and 900 barrels. Visits by individuals and groups are by appointment, mornings and afternoons. English and French are spoken.

Varal, Bodegas (Baños de Ebro, Alavesa, ☎ 941 123 321) was founded in 1987 and is a modern, fully-equipped bodega with 45ha (111 acres) of vineyards surrounding the bodega and beautiful views of the surrounding countryside. Varal produce a *joven* red under the ***Trujalero*** label containing 90 per cent Tempranillo and 10 per cent Viura. Individual and group visits (mornings and afternoons) by appointment.

Velázquez Bodegas (Cenicero, Alta) is a medium-size family bodega with premises completed in 1973. They have over 2,000 barrels and 45ha (111 acres) of vineyards and also use bought-in grapes and wine. Velázquez produce only red *crianza*, *reserva* and *gran reserva* wines (80 per cent Tempranillo, 15 per cent Mazuelo and 5 per cent Viura), mainly under the ***Monte Velaz*** label, all of which have a good balance between the American oak taste and the fruit. Other labels used include ***La Rendición***, ***La Túnica*** and ***Las Hilanderas***.

Velasco Barrios, Angel (Sotés, Alta, ☎/🖷 941 441 785) was founded in 1973 and has concrete cellars containing 35 barrels, concrete tanks (from 1970) and modern stainless steel tanks (installed in 1980). The ***Castillo de Promedano*** *joven* range includes red, white and rosé wines using Tempranillo, Garnacha and Viura. Daily visits (individuals and groups) by appointment.

Viguera Gómez, José-María (Logroño, Alta, ☎ 941 236 980) was founded in 1770, although the cut-stone building was built in 1521 and was previously the home of the wife of General Espartero (one time Regent and head of the Spanish government). The underground cellar has vaulted ceilings. Visits by groups are by appointment. There is a restaurant, *Reja Dorada*, and English and French are spoken.

Viña Ijalba, *Provir* (Logroño, Alta, ☎ 941 261 100, 🖷 941 261 118) was founded in 1975 and is a modern bodega (built in

1991), which was dramatically different from that of the classic bodega, although the *avant-garde* design is coupled with the latest technology. The vines are planted at just 3,400 per hectare, with the strictly controlled low-yield of less than 4,500kg (9,920lb) per hectare ensuring top quality wines. The vineyards are also tended ecologically using manure only – no herbicides or synthesised plant protection agents are used and the whole vinification process is carried out without the addition of chemical products or additional irrigation. Traditional burnt sulphur is the only agent used and even then only in strictly controlled optimal quantities. All wines are made from grapes grown in their own vineyards.

The original vineyards were planted in old disused gravel pits and now cover 70ha (173 acres), while the 2,500 American oak barrels are housed in temperature and humidity-controlled cellars. Ijalba is an exciting, relatively new bodega producing distinctive style wines sold in unusual long thin, heavy bottles, which have a patent on the UV-resistant glass designed to protect the wine from light, air and temperature. Quality, ecologically-produced wines are the key-note of this bodega, where even the labels and boxes use heavy-metal-free inks and the capsules are tin (not lead).

Ijalba produced the very first Graciano varietal wine in Rioja, a rare, young fruity red Graciano. There is also a Tempranillo red *joven* **Solferino** (Spanish for a reddish-purple hue) made by carbonic maceration, whole-grape fermentation from grapes that are pressed by foot. **Múrice** (an old Spanish name for crimson) is a rounded, full-bodied, fruity *crianza*, using 90 per cent Tempranillo, 5 per cent Mazuelo and 5 per cent Graciano grapes. All grapes are estate grown and subjected to one of two winemaking methods, one using whole grapes and the other crushed grapes without stems (under strictly controlled conditions). The two wines are then blended and aged for twelve months.

Ijalba also make a delicate white 100 per cent Viura (estate grown) labelled **Genoli** (a yellow hue formerly used in paintings) and a fresh, distinctive joven rosé called **Aloque** (the Spanish name for a light red hue) containing 80 per cent Garnacha, 10 per cent Tempranillo and 10 per cent Mazuelo. The *joven* **Livor** is a deep red colour typical of young red wines, full flavoured and fruity, using 90 per cent Tempranillo and 5 per cent each of Graciano and Mazuelo.

Two different winemaking methods are again used. The first involves whole grape carbonic maceration and the wine is racked to separate the must from the skins, foot-pressed and then undergoes controlled temperature fermentation, while in the second method de-stalking takes place before crushing followed by controlled fermentation in stainless steel tanks. The resulting wines are then blended in equal quantities and stabilised before bottling.

Ijalba reserva, made from 90 per cent Tempranillo and 10 per cent Graciano, has two years in American oak barrels and is racked eight times, followed by two years in bottle to produce a delicious full-bodied, smooth and spicy red. Last, but not least, the *Ijalba reserva especial*, containing 50 per cent Graciano and 50 per cent Tempranillo, is a rounded, quality, delicious red. Visits are by appointment on weekday mornings and afternoons, with optional wine tasting courses given by experts. English and French are spoken.

Viña Paterna (Elciego, Alavesa, ☏ 941 606 277, 🖷 941 142 347), founded in 1984, is housed in a 150-year-old mansion (with an attractive 17th century underground structure) and has 12ha (30 acres) of vineyards. Their *Viña Lur* is a smooth, fruity red *joven* wine using 80 per cent Tempranillo, 8 per cent Viura and a 12 per cent blend of Graciano, Garnacha and Mazuelo. Individual and group (maximum 15 people) visits are by appointment daily, except Sunday. English and French are spoken.

Viña Salceda (Elciego, Alavesa, ☏ 941 606 125, 🖷 941 606 069) was founded in 1969 and located between Cenicero in the Rioja Alta and Elciego in the Rioja Alavesa. The main building was constructed in 1972 in typical Basque rural style with a large covered porch and is situated in the middle of the picturesque 15ha (37 acres) estate. It belongs to a large group of shareholders who own 30ha (74 acres) of vineyards, although these provide only a small percentage of the bodega's requirements, with the bulk of grapes and wines being bought-in. *Viña Salceda* has 6,500 barrels, used for ageing, together with stainless steel fermentation tanks installed in 1974. The red *Viña Salceda crianza* is of good quality, while the **Conde**

de la Salceda gran reserva is fuller, richer and more elegant (both are predominantly Tempranillo). Individual and group visits are by appointment on weekday mornings and afternoons. English is spoken.

Viña Valoria (Logroño, Alta, ☉ 941 204 059, 📠 941 204 155) was founded in 1989 and has 25ha (62 acres) of vineyards and 800 barrels. The quality aged reds tend to be 70 per cent Tempranillo, 20 per cent Mazuelo and 10 per cent Graciano, sold under the elaborate *Viña Valoria*. There is also a *joven* range of wines.

Viña Villabueno (Villabueno, Alavesa, ☉ 941 609 086, 📠 941 609 261) was founded in 1987 and built on an incline with brick facings of original design. The cellars contain 5,500 barrels. They produce good red *crianza* and *reserva* wines labelled *Viña Izadi*, normally using 90 per cent Tempranillo plus Mazuelo and Graciano. Visits are arranged daily by appointment (individuals and groups). They also have a hotel with fully-equipped, air-conditioned bedrooms, a games room and a 50-seat restaurant.

Viñedos de Aldeanueva, S. Coop (Aldeanueva, Baja, ☉ 941 163 039, 📠 941 163 585, ✉ aldeanueva@inx3.redestb.es) was founded in 1956, with a new building added in 1974 which is in total contrast to the older one. This is the largest bodega in Rioja, making its own wine and doing so with outstanding oeonological technology and commitment to quality. They have an enormous 2,500ha (6,177 acres) of vineyards and 7,000 barrels. Morning and afternoon visits are by appointment (individuals and groups) daily, except Sunday. There is also a shop and – bullfights! English and French are spoken (but not by the bulls).

Viñedos del Contino (Laserna, Alavesa, ☉ 941 600 201, 📠 941 121 114) was founded in 1974 by *CVNE* and a group of private individuals. It is a small, château-style, single-vineyard estate with 60ha (148 acres) and 1,650 barrels, half American and half French. The vines are planted in an indentation in the hills running down to the banks of the River Ebro, and Contino is one of the earliest bodegas in the Rioja Alavesa to commence the harvest (*vendimia*) and has a low yield per hectare. The red *Contino reserva* is deep coloured and concentrated, with plenty of body and a vanilla bouquet. The bodega uses its own grapes

(85 per cent Tempranillo, 9 per cent Mazuelo, 5 per cent Graciano and 1 per cent Garnacha) for this quality *reserva*, which has two years in oak and two in bottle. Individual and group visits are by appointment on weekday mornings and afternoons (closed in August). English is spoken.

Viñedos y Bodegas de la Marquesa, SMS (Villabuena, Alavesa), see SMS Bodega, Bodegas de la Marquesa, SMS, who produce the delicious and limited production *Valserrano*.

Vinícola Davalillo, S. Coop (San Asensio, Alta, ☾/🖷 941 457 133) was founded in 1987 and is situated next to the *Monastery of La Estrella*, with beautiful views of the Ebro River and the castles of San Vicente and Davalillo. The bodega has 265 barrels. The *Covilda, Señorío de la Estrella* and *Valprado* labels are used for their ranges of red *crianzas*, and red, white and rosé *jóvenes*. Tempranillo is used for all the reds, Viura for the whites and Garnacha for the rosés. Visits are by appointment.

Vinícola Riojanas de Alcanadre, S. Coop (Alcanadre, Baja, ☾ 941 165 036, 🖷 941 165 289) was founded in 1957 and has a huge 650ha (1,606 acres) of vineyards. The original building (containing concrete tanks) was enlarged in 1990 and modern stainless steel tanks installed. Two of their best-known labels are *Aradón*, a *joven* range and *Barzagoso,* a *crianza* containing 70 per cent Tempranillo and 15 per cent each of Mazuelo and Garnacha, and aged in American oak. Visits are by appointment daily except Sunday (French is spoken).

Viños Iradier (Abalos, Alta, ☾/🖷 941 334 251) was founded in 1983 and built in contemporary style. They use whole grape carbonic maceration for their quality *joven* range of wines. The *Iradier* label is used for the red, which contains 85 per cent Tempranillo and 15 per cent Viura, while the white is 100 per cent Viura and the rosé 65 per cent Garnacha and 35 per cent Viura. Visits for individuals by appointment.

Virgen del Valle, Bodegas (Samaniego, Alavesa, ☾ 941 609 033, 🖷 941 619 106) was formed in 1987. It uses selected bought-in grapes and its wines are aged in 1,000 barrels in their 20m (66ft) deep 17th century cellars. The *Cincel crianza* is a light, well-balanced red using 85 per cent Tempranillo and 15 per cent Garnacha, the same as the *gran reserva* and *reserva* which have more body. The young 100 per cent Tempranillo red ***Chocante*** *joven* is produced by carbonic maceration, while the white is 100 per cent Viura and the rosé 100 per cent Garnacha. Individual and group visits by appointment.

Viteri Muro, Pedro (Lapuebla de Labarca, Alavesa, ☏ 941 607 123) was founded in 1978 and has 15ha (37 acres) of vineyards and 20 barrels. Individual and group visits are by appointment on weekdays between 9am and 6pm. They also have a shop.

Zugober (Lapuebla de Labarca, Alavesa, ☏ 941 127 228, 🖷 941 127 281) was founded in 1988 in a new building with stainless steel facilities and 110 barrels. Their range of red *crianzas* and red, white and rosé *jóvenes* use the labels of ***Bringi, Buyango*** and ***Belezos***. The reds are a varying blend of Tempranillo coupled with a small percentage of Mazuelo and Garnacha. Visits by individuals and groups are by appointment on weekdays from 9am to 2pm. English and French are spoken.

Torrecilla

3.

VISITING RIOJA

La Rioja not only produces some of the best wines in the world, but it is also a fascinating region to visit, offering spectacular unspoilt countryside and mountain scenery. It is an inviting, compact area with a profusion of ancient villages and towns, a wealth of art, culture and history, numerous boisterous festivals, and a wide choice of excellent hotels and restaurants.

Rioja has a long culinary tradition and is celebrated for its wholesome country fare including a huge variety of fresh fruit and vegetables from local market gardens, and succulent meat and game from the region's farms, with lamb and kid particular specialities. The Atlantic is a rich source of fresh seafood and fish, well supplemented by trout and other fresh-water fish from local rivers. Seasoned liberally with excellent value for money and Rioja's celebrated wines, you have the perfect table to satisfy the most demanding gourmet.

However, the pleasures do not stop there – long after you return home you will be able to re-savour the delights of Rioja as you reminisce about tasting (and buying) your wines, with the familiar refrain, "do you remember when we drank that . . ." – far better than any holiday snaps. Visit now before other tourists spoil it!

Getting There

La Rioja is easily accessible on excellent roads from France and other regions of Spain, by ferry from Britain (via Bilbao, Santander and the Channel ports), by air to Bilbao (where you can hire a car or take a domestic flight to Logroño) and even by train. The nearest international airport to Rioja is Bilbao, which has direct flights to most major European cities, including London's Heathrow and Stanstead airports, the laer being considerably cheaper. Cars can be hired at the airport and in less than two hours of easy driving, mostly on motorways, you will be in the heart of Rioja. An increasing number of tour operators offer holidays in Rioja including trips to the bodegas to dine, taste and buy wines directly, which is an excellent introduction to this interesting region.

However, the independence of travelling to Rioja in your own car has the enormous advantage of being able to return laden with delicious wines at bargain prices. Travelling by car through France can also actually work out more cost-effective than either a fly-drive deal or a ferry to Spain, which, although saving some 1,000km (620mi) of driving through France, is not cheap. You may also wish to bear in mind that the Bay of Biscay can be an unpleasant place for poor sailors!

Ferries from Britain to Spain

To save the drive through France, you can take a twice-weekly crossing on the large cruise ferries operating between Britain and Spain. P&O sail from Portsmouth to Bilbao (the ferry port is actually at Santurtzi, about 13km/8mi north-west of the city centre) and Brittany Ferries cross to Santander from Portsmouth (Plymouth in winter). They have mini-cruise facilities and luxury cabins are available, although the cost of cabins is not included in the price for the vehicle and passengers.

Onward travel by road (use Michelin map 442): From Santander take the E70/A67 motorway (*autovía*) to Bilbao (80km/50mi) and then the A68 towards Vitoria/Gasteiz, and at junction 5 follow the signs to Logroño and take junction 9 for Haro (Haro is 80km/50mi from Bilbao, while Logroño is 125km/78mi). From Santurtzi (Bilbao's port) take the road sign-posted to Bilbao and you quickly find yourself on the A68 motorway, and in well under two hours you will be in the either Haro or Logroño sitting outside a cafe enjoying a glass of Rioja.

> **Take care to observe the speed limits in La Rioja, particularly when in a 50kph (31mph) zone, as you can be fined 20,000 pesetas on the spot for speeding!**

Travelling from Britain by Car via France

It is possible, with an early morning start, to travel from the Channel ports to Rioja in one day, although this would be tiring and is not advisable. It is far better to take a little more time and consider the journey as part of your holiday. Dover to Calais is an extremely flexible way of travelling, with a frequent ferry service (every half an hour at peak times), quick and easy loading, and a fast crossing (90 minutes). Alternatively, Eurotunnel trains take 35 minutes from Folkestone to Coquelles (near Calais) and run every 15 minutes at peak times.

Once in France you are straight on to the motorway (*autoroute*) to Paris (see the box below for the best route to negotiate Paris) and then on to Bordeaux, where you follow the signs for Arcachon and San Sebastián in northern Spain. Although you pay tolls on the *autoroutes* as far as Bordeaux, you can travel quickly at 130kph (81mph), and with service stations at regular intervals, there is no need to make a detour to find petrol, food, drink or toilets. This route also saves the cost of an extra night in a hotel and the journey takes no longer than the ferry crossing to Bilbao or Santander.

> **Route through Paris: Approaching Paris on the A1 *Autoroute*, take the first exit after Charles de Gaulle Airport on to the A3, (Bordeaux and Paris Este). Follow the signs to Lyons, Metz and Nancy and take the A4 (to Créteil) then the A86, still signposted to Créteil. Follow the signpost to Bordeaux on to the N186A, then the A6 (A10) to Orléans and you are through Paris and on your way to Rioja.**

Alternatively, if you prefer to avoid the *autoroutes*, you can take a leisurely drive through France on A-roads (prefixed 'N' for 'national') and after an overnight stop, arrive in Rioja in time for lunch next day. There is a wide choice of scheduled car ferry services from Britain operating from the ports of Dover, Folkestone, Newhaven, Plymouth, Poole, Portsmouth and Weymouth (plus the Irish ports of Cork and Rosslare). The major ferry companies are P&O Stena from Dover to Calais, P&O from Portsmouth to Cherbourg and Le Havre, with the Catamaran to Cherbourg the quickest crossing, taking just 2 hours and 30 minutes.

Brittany ferries cross from Portsmouth to Caen and St. Malo, Plymouth to Roscoff and Santander, Poole to Cherbourg, and Cork to Roscoff. Hoverspeed operates a hovercraft service

▲ *La Rioja's rich gastronomy*

► *Characteristic Riojan stone house in Cenicero*

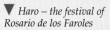

▼ *Haro – the festival of Rosario de los Faroles*

Wine labels

Young Wine: Un-aged wines in their first or second year.

Crianza: Wines at least two years old which have spent a minimum of one year ageing in oak casks.

Reserva: Carefully selected wines which have spent a minimum of three years ageing in oak barrels and bottles. At least one year to have been in oak casks.

Gran Reserva: Wines of exceptional vintages which have spent a minimum of two years ageing in oak casks and three in bottles.

Liquid gold

► *Master Wine-taster*

▼ *Wines ageing in oak barrels*

▲ Typical view of Riojan vineyards with Briones in the background

◄ Grape-picker

▼ Ancient manuscript in Yuso Monestry

between Dover and Calais plus Folkestone to Boulogne. A larger, Hoverspeed superseacat service operates from Newhaven to Dieppe, and Condor operates a fast service (five hours) from Weymouth to St. Malo. Comprehensive free timetables are published by all the ferry companies and are available from travel agents. Note that some ferry companies stopped publishing fares in their brochures in 2000, although this decision may be reversed after numerous complaints. Meanwhile you will need to telephone ferry companies for prices (see **Appendix H**).

DISTANCES

From – To	km/miles
Calais – San Sebastián	1,110km/690mi
Calais – Paris	282km/175mi
Paris – Bordeaux	538kn/335mi
Bordeaux – San Sebastián	290km/180mi
Caen – San Sebastián	837km/520mi
Cherbourg – San Sebastián	861km/535mi
LeHavre – San Sebastián	845km/525mi
Roscoff – San Sebastián	885km/550mi
St. Malo – San Sebastián	772km/480mi
San Sebastián – Haro	145km/90mi
San Sebastián – Logroño	177km/110mi
Laguardia – Haro	21km/13mi
Logroño – Arnedo	64km/40mi
Logroño – Bilbao	125km/78mi
Logroño – Laguardia	21km/13mi
Logroño – Cenicero	21km/13mi
Logroño – Santo Domingo de la Calzada	40km/25mi
Logroño – San Sebastián	170km/106mi
Haro – Bilbao	80km/50mi
Haro – Logroño	42km/26mi

All distances are via the shortest or fastest routes.

> **"O thou invisible spirit of wine."**
> **Shakespeare (Othello)**

Main Towns

The main towns of La Rioja are Haro and Logroño, both of which are not to be missed. Logroño is the regional capital and administrative centre and the largest town in Rioja, situated roughly in the centre of the region, while Haro is a relatively small town in the Rioja Alta, which is the centre of Rioja's wine industry. Haro and Logroño, both equally interesting and important in their own right, are totally different in character and deservedly the starting point for a visit to the region. Due to the great rivalry between these towns, they are described below in alphabetical order!

Haro

Haro (pop. 9,500) is a small, attractive town situated on the N232 to Vitoria 42km (26mi) from Logroño, and generally the starting point for a visit to Rioja. It dates back to the 10th century and has been the centre of viticultural activity in Rioja for centuries. It is built on the sides and top of a hill on the southern slopes of the Obarenes mountains at the mouth of the River Tirón, where a lighthouse used to flash its warning to vessels joining from the River Ebro. It is a small, compact town encouraging visitors to stroll around and enjoy its many attractions. Your first stop should be the friendly tourist office, which can provide you with a wealth of information about Haro and La Rioja.

The area known as *La Herradura* (the horseshoe) contains a number of excellent restaurants, cafes and bars offering mouth-watering *tapas*. In the nearby central square, the Plaza de la Paz, you can have breakfast (*desayuno*) of freshly squeezed orange juice, a selection of fresh, home-made *tapas*, tea or coffee, or even a glass of wine, for a few hundred pesetas.

Meanwhile sit back and relax and admire the 16th century *Casa de Paternina* and the late 18th century town hall. This large square is flanked by stylish *fin de siècle* buildings with characteristic balconies, radiating off to a rabbit warren of narrow side streets. One of these, the Calle Santo Tomás, leads to the lovely old Gothic *Church of Santo Tomás*, which has an Herreran style south portal, delicately carved by Felipe de Vigarni in 1516, a Gothic nave and a baroque altarpiece.

In the middle of the last century when phylloxera devastated the vineyards in France, the Bordeaux vintners came to Rioja to buy wine and established their own wine bodegas in Haro. In addition to buying directly from the producers at the *bodegas*, there is an even wider selection of wines available in the local wine shops, also called *bodegas*, where you can stock up on wine and local gastronomic specialities.

Special offers at irresistible prices make a compelling argument for taking your car to Haro and loading the boot with a mouth-watering selection of wines. These local wine shops offer an almost unbelievable variety of Riojan wines and in Calle Sto. Tomás there are a number of excellent wine shops, including **La Hermandad Vinícola (Comercial Vinícola Riojana)**, with English-speaking staff who are extremely helpful and a mine of information about local wines. They stock a wide range of Riojan wines in ideal conditions (all lying down!) and they also have an interesting selection of speciality foods, olive (and other) oil and wine vinegars. There are many other good bodegas and gift shops in Haro including, for example, **Cristaleriás Salgueiro** at 32 Conde de Haro, where you can choose from an array of interesting gifts, including reasonably-priced wine glasses (*copas*) in which to taste and savour your Riojan wine.

While in Rioja, wine lovers will not want to miss the absorbing *Wine Museum of La Rioja* at the *Estación de Viticultura y Enológica*, a government wine laboratory. This museum provides a fascinating insight into the region and Riojan wine production, with one floor dedicated to local cultural activities and traditions, another illustrating all the activities necessary for the production and sale of Riojan wines, and a further floor showing the effect of soils and climate on wine growing. At Briñas, on the N124 road north to Vitoria, there is another wine museum displaying artefacts and offering wine tastings and another chance to buy wine.

Haro's Bodegas

The Barrio de la Estación (railway station quarter) houses a number of historical bodegas including *Bodegas Bilbaínas, Berceo, CVNE, La Rioja Alta, López Heredia-Viña Tondonia* and *Muga* – all of which are legendary Riojan wine names. Listed below are a number of bodegas in Haro, which welcome visitors by appointment. See **Chapter 2** (Rioja's Bodegas) for further information.

Berceo Bodegas (32, Cuevas, ✆ 941 310 744) is situated in the traditional winemaking quarter. It was founded in 1872 and has cellars dating back to the Middle Ages, which have been declared part of the historical and artistic heritage of the town. They are one of the oldest bodegas in Rioja and the only vertical one left. Visits for individuals and groups are by appointment (French is spoken).

Bilbaínas Bodegas (3, Barrio de la Estación, ✆ 941 310 147) has a main building dating back to the 19th century in cut-stone with a unique façade and large cellars containing 13,000 barrels. Bilbaínas were the pioneers in Rioja of the *méthode champenoise* for making Cavas. They welcome individual visitors on weekdays by appointment (English and French are spoken).

Carlos Serres Bodegas (40, Av. Santo Domingo, ✆ 941 310 294) was founded in 1896. Weekday tastings are from 8am to 6pm (both English and French are spoken).

CVNE, Compañía Vinícola del Norte de España (21, Av. Costa del Vino, Barrio de la Estación, ✆ 941 304 800), was founded in 1879. They have 19th century warehouses and cellars with an 1895 Malvoisin pasteurizer. Visits for individuals and groups are by appointment on weekday mornings and afternoons (avoid 1 to 3pm). English, French and German are spoken.

Florentino de Lecanda (36, Cuevas, ✆ 941 303 477) was founded in 1965 and is a traditional Riojan bodega in natural stone and limestone, situated in the traditional winemaking quarter of Haro. Visits are weekday mornings and afternoons.

Gómez Cruzado Bodegas (6, Av. De Vizcaya, ☏ 941 312 502) was founded in 1886 and the cut-stone, barrel-ageing chambers and oak fermentation vats date back to the original construction. Visits daily mornings and afternoons except Sundays (English is spoken).

La Rioja Alta (Av. De Vizcaya, ☏ 941 310 346) is family owned (founded 1890) and produces quality wines from their 300ha (741 acres) of vineyards and 30,000 oak barrels. Visiting is on weekday mornings and English is spoken.

Martínez Lacuesta Bodegas (71, La Ventilla, ☏ 941 310 050) was founded in 1895 and has three stone buildings dating from the late 19th century and other more modern buildings. Individual and group visits on weekday mornings from June to September from 9am to 2pm, and both mornings and afternoons from May to October (they are closed in August). French is spoken.

Muga Bodegas (Barrio de la Estación, ☏ 948 670 050) were founded in 1932 and are housed in a classic stone building dating from 1856. It is a traditional bodega using oak in all stages of vinification and ageing. Visits are mainly mornings.

Paternina Federico Bodegas (11, Av. Santo Domingo, ☏ 941 310 550) was founded in 1896 and the contemporary bodega stands out for its *Banda Azul* building (the name of one of its most successful wines). Visits are weekday mornings and afternoons, including Saturdays.

Ramón Bilbao Bodegas (34, Av. Santo Domingo, ☏ 941 310 295) was founded in 1924 and is of typical Riojan architecture. Weekday visits (mornings and afternoons).

Rioja Santiago Bodegas (Barrio de la Estación, ☏ 941 310 200), founded in 1870, is the third-oldest bodega in Rioja. Visits by individuals and groups are by appointment on weekday mornings from 9am to 2pm. English is spoken.

Rubí Bodegas (Ctra. Anguciana, ☏ 941 310 937) was founded in 1989 and has contemporary architecture in concrete and cut-stone. Visits are by appointment on weekday mornings and afternoons, except for June to September, when they are mornings only.

> Every day at a cost of just a few hundred
> pesetas, a local train wends its way between
> Haro and Logroño through the attractive
> countryside dotted with vineyards. This saves
> you having to drive and allows you to indulge in
> your favourite pastime – drinking Rioja.
> However, although the train stops at
> Fuenmayor, Cenicero and Briones, your ticket
> does not allow you to break your journey.

Logroño

Logroño (pop. 130,000) is the capital of the province of La
Rioja and its administrative and commercial centre. Situated on
the banks of the River Ebro, it is the largest and most modern
town in Rioja, with hundreds of interesting and elegant shops to
tempt and satisfy the most ardent shopaholic! The helpful
tourist office is located in the Espolón, which is a focal point
for locals and tourists alike, with its leafy plane trees offering
much needed shade and seats where you can sit and rest your
weary feet and watch the world go by. Wandering around
Logroño provides numerous opportunities to stop for *tapas* and
a glass of Rioja in this vibrant wine city, with its pavements
inset with tiles bearing wine motifs. There is a wealth of
restaurants, all with impressive Riojan wine lists and the best of
Riojan cuisine.

Logroño has been a settlement since ancient times, with its
stone and iron bridges across the River Ebro (embodied in the
town's coat of arms) providing a protective barrier against
enemies. It is here that the *Pilgrims' Way to Santiago de
Compostela* crosses the River Ebro to join up with the old
Roman road for the historic journey. During excavations,
human remains were found within the city walls and in caves
on the nearby slopes inhabited during the Middle Ages (later
put to good use as wine cellars). Cantabria Hill, just outside
Logroño on the N111, is one of two local archaeological sites
where Celtiberian, Roman and medieval remains have also

been found (other remains have been found at Varea on the N232).

The old town was originally walled and in the area stretching from the river to the Paseo del Espolón remains of the walls (*muros*) can still be seen, including the *Muro del Carmen*, the *Muro de la Mata* and the *Muro de Cervantes*. The still fully intact *Revellín Gate* is set in the old walls in an area where many churches and mansions were built, and is on the *Pilgrims Way* out of the city. *San Bartolomé Church*, situated at the most easterly part of the walls, is believed to have been a defensive position and is now a national monument. It is a beautiful stone building with a spectacular façade and three two-span naves and an aligned transept with a typical 12th century triple back. The central part of this impressive edifice is semi-circular and covered by a pointed vault and dome (the square sides also have pointed vaults). Visits are permitted during services and the cool interior is a welcome relief from the summer heat.

The twin towers of the 16th century cathedral church of *Santa María de la Redonda* are prominent on the city's skyline, particularly from the north. It is a three-nave building with the towers and façade (completed in 1762) in beautiful dressed stone. The impressive organ and choir, together with their paintings (one by Michelangelo) make *La Redonda* well worth a visit. Unlike most other churches, where visits are permitted only during services, here you are welcome anytime from 7.45am to 1pm or between 6.30 and 9pm.

Santa María de la Redonda and the older churches of *San Bartolomé* and *Santa María de Palacio* were originally part of a palace that Alfonso VII presented to the Order of the Holy Sepulchre at the beginning of the 11th century. The historic *Santiago el Real Church*, situated on the *Pilgrims' Way*, is an imposing single-nave building with a 17th century façade containing a statue of Santiago Matamoros. Inside the church the altarpiece shows scenes from the Saint's life and there is also an image of Nuestra Señora de la Esperanza, the city's patron.

Calle Mayor, an important thoroughfare running parallel to the River Ebro and crossing the city from east to west, boasts the *Imperial Santa María de Palacio* church with an impressive pyramid Gothic spire. The main part of the church was constructed in the 13th century, although building commenced in the 12th century and was finally finished only in the 17th century – the builders *were not* paid a productivity bonus! It could also explain why this dressed stone building of three-spanned naves has two octagonal sides and a square middle!

> **If you would like an English or French-speaking guide to escort you around the town, *Carmen Merino Lozano*, who owns a travel agency at 17 Calle Chile (☎ 941 201 172, ⊜ 941 214 654), will be happy to show you old Logroño during her 2 to 5pm break. But do not forget to make an appointment in advance!**

Along the Calle Mayor are a number of old buildings (complete with wine cellars) from the 16th to 19th centuries and at one end is the old *Merced c*onvent, now restored and converted into the *Parliament of La Rioja*, while next door the old tobacco factory has become the public library. In San Augustín Square there is the beautiful 18th century mansion of *General Espartero* (1793-1879 – one time Regent and head of the Spanish government), housing the absorbing *Museum of La Rioja*. It can be visited from Tuesdays to Saturdays from 10am to 2pm and 4 to 8pm, and from 11.30am to 2pm on Sundays and public holidays (it is closed on Mondays). Nearby is one of Spain's most attractive market buildings, built in 1930, and the recently re-modelled *Breton de los Herreros* theatre, named after a famous Spanish playwright. The city hall, although a modern building (designed by Rafael Moneo and completed in 1980), complements Logroño's many handsome old buildings and is admired as a fine example of modern design.

The old centre is transformed at night into a noisy, vibrant, meeting place, crammed with people seriously intent on enjoying themselves in true Riojan style. Excellent restaurants and *tapas* bars abound in Calle Laurel, each with their own specialities. Although they typically serve good young Riojan wines in a small tumbler (*chiquito*), which complement the tempting *tapas* sitting invitingly on the bar counters, there is also an abundance of older vintages to positively drool over just waiting to be enjoyed. Wander from bar to bar, 'drinking in' not only the wines but also the vibrant atmosphere, while sampling local specialities such as the delicious butter-fried, garlic mushrooms (*champis*) in the Angel or *zapatillas* (ham on bread shaped like a slipper) in La Méngula. To round off your evening, why not try the tempting Champagne lemon sorbet (*sorbete de champán y limón*) at La Casita and finally a cappuccino under the stars at the Parliament Café – a treat awaits you.

Logroño's *tapas* bars, excellent restaurants, lively festivities, beautiful churches, bodegas and lively ambience, add up to a town definitely not to be missed.

Logroño's Bodegas

Of the nine bodegas in an around Logroño (listed below) all require visitors to make appointments and most speak English and/or French. See **Chapter 2** (Rioja's Bodegas) for further information.

Bodegas Bretón y Cía (20, Av.Lope de Vega, ② 941 212 225) was founded in 1985 and produces reds and barrel-fermented white wines. Visits are Mondays to Saturdays between 9am and 1.30pm and from 4.30 to 7.30pm. English and French are spoken.

Bodegas Campo Viejo (3, Gustavo Adolfo Bécquer, ② 941 279 900) was formed in 1961. Bodegas y Bebidas, one of the largest firms in Rioja, have a controlling interest. Visits are weekday mornings from 8.30am to 12.30pm and afternoons from 2.30 to 5pm (English and French are spoken).

Bodegas Franco-Españolas (2, Cabo Noval, ② 941 251 300) were founded in 1890 and are a traditional bodega built in French style, overlooking the Puente de Hierro (bridge). The whole bodega is lovingly maintained and there are extensive underground cellars. There are weekday visits and English and French are spoken.

Bodegas Marqués de Murrieta (Km 403, Ctra. Zaragossa, Finca Ygay, ② 941 258 100) was founded in 1872 and is a much respected bodega. There are three stone buildings with one representing the old Ygay castle and the estate, which picturesquely surrounds the bodega, covers 290ha (717 acres). Weekday visits mornings and afternoons.

Bodegas Olarra (Polígono de Cantabria, ☎ 941 235 299) is a strikingly modern building with a unique style of brick-faced, exposed concrete and Arabic tiles. They have weekday visits and English is spoken.

Bodegas Ontañon (Km 3, Ctra Zaragossa, ☎ 941 234 200) is situated on the outskirts of Logroño on the N232 (ten minutes from the centre) and is a large, new bodega incorporating works of art (e.g. windows, statues and paintings) by a talented local artist. English is spoken.

Finca La Grajera Comunidad Autónoma de la Rioja (Km 6, Ctra. de Burgos, ☎ 941 291 263) was founded in 1977 and has visits from 8am to 4pm. They will also show you the Agricultural Research and Development Centre experimental plots.

Viguera Gómez (19, Ruavieja, ☎ 941 236 980) was founded in 1770, incorporating a building dating from 1521 with an underground cellar and vaulted stone ceilings. They have their own restaurant, *Reja Dorada*, and the house was formerly the home of the wife of General Espartero. French is spoken.

Viña Ijalba (Km 1, Ctra. Pamplona, ☎ 941 261 100) was founded in 1975 on old gravel pits. They use their own ecologically grown grapes to produce a distinctive and excellent quality range of wines. Visits are weekday mornings and afternoons, with optional wine tasting courses given by experts. English and French are spoken.

Logroño is home to the *Consejo Regulador* (Regulating Council, 52 Calle Estambrera) for Riojan wine production, which celebrates its 75th anniversary in the year 2000. You can visit their offices to obtain information and buy gifts from the interesting souvenir shop, and also arrange to participate in one-day wine courses.

Other Interesting Towns & Sites

ABALOS (Rioja Alta), east of Haro, is a picturesque village dominated by the Sierra de Cantabria mountains. Its fascinating narrow streets contain many 17th and 18th century stone buildings, embossed coats of arms, an old palace and a beautiful ornate 16th century church with a baroque tower containing a priceless altarpiece. Abalos is surrounded by vineyards and is the home of seven bodegas, including *Bodegas Real Divisa*, one of the oldest in Europe.

ALDEANUEVO DE EBRO (Rioja Baja) is a busy and thriving town with a prominent shoe industry. The local church has an attractive 16th century altarpiece. The name of the town is a total contradiction. It is not an *aldea* (a hamlet), it is not *nueva* (new), although it no doubt was at one time, and it is not even on the River Ebro – other than that the name describes the town exactly!

ALFARO (Rioja Baja) is an attractive, small Roman town on the River Ebro and the furthest point reached by the shallow-draught boats of the Phoenician maritime traders around 1,000BC. The name is derived from El Faro (Spanish for 'lighthouse') and the town was an important protected frontier between Castile and the Kingdom of Navarre. Alfaro boasts a number of beautiful old churches, some elegant baronial houses, seven bodegas and the world's largest white stork colony on a single building (beware of  droppings!). Bulls play an important part in the fiestas that take place from mid-August to the beginning of September. The *Hotel Palacios*, conveniently located next to *Bodegas Palacios Remondo*, has an excellent restaurant, plus a wine and fossil museum.

ANGUIANO (Rioja Alta) is a village situated in the beautiful, wooded Sierra de la Demanda mountains, where famous dancers on stilts take part in local fiestas around the 22nd July and on the last Sunday in September. The Monasteries of Suso and Yuso at San Millán de La Cogolla, Cañas, Valvanera and Nájera are all located within around 16km (10mi) of Anguiano and not to be missed. See the **Bodega and Monastery Route** on page 141.

ARNEDILLO (Rioja Baja), surrounded by mountains, is a celebrated spa town for rheumatism and bone disorders. It is also the home of the Château-like *Santuario Vinícola Riojano* bodega, built around a 300-year-old mill on the banks of the River Cidacos.

ARNEDO (Rioja Baja), situated in a red sandstone gorge on the left bank of the River Cidacos, is famous for its spa, with its clean, odourless waters remain at a steady 52.5°F (11.4°C). The mud, a blend of the spa waters and local clay, contains minerals claimed to be beneficial for the treatment of arthritis, gout and rheumatism, among other ailments. It is also extremely relaxing and acts as a vasodilator, opening up the blood vessels to help soothe aching muscles after over indulgence in the many active leisure pursuits available locally. Other attractions include ornate churches with rich baroque interiors, a *Footwear Museum*, interesting walks and the local Forestry Board's feeding area, where you can watch *Leonard Vultures*.

AUSEJO (Rioja Baja) is a fortified hill town dominated by a 13th century castle. The old town centre is a jumble of winding streets, beneath which are a labyrinth of underground cellars and tunnels. Ausejo is noted for its mushrooms as well as its wine.

BALCON de la RIOJA (Rioja Alavesa), close to Navaridas, is a spectacular 1,100m (3,609ft) vantage point overlooking the Rioja Alavesa and the River Ebro valley, where most of the countryside is planted with vines. It is a popular picnic area where fresh mountain water gushes from a fascinating tap – however, it is prone to flies in hot weather, which may spoil your picnic but not the stunning views.

BRIÑAS (Rioja Alta) is an historic and artistic village just 3km from Haro on the N124 to Vitoria/Gasteiz, boasting a medieval bridge across the River Ebro and claiming to have more mansions than anywhere else in the region. In the old Plaza de la Constitución there is the impressive 16th century

Church of the Asunción, containing a beautiful 17th century altarpiece, while nearby is a wall fountain with vaulted pipes dating from the 12th century and a cross from 1569. Briñas is known as the 'wine cellar village' due to the many ventilation shafts from its wine cellars below – when the wines are fermenting a wonderful aroma permeates the whole village. In the centre, the excellent *Hospedería Señorío de Briñas* hotel is olde-worlde, with modern facilities and friendly hosts.

BRIONES (Rioja Alta), east of Haro, is a small, picturesque hilltop town with panoramic views of the River Ebro valley, a statuesque church and largely intact medieval walls. Storks arrive every year to nest on the church spire, as they do in many other parts of Rioja, and according to local winegrowers the date of their arrival is an indication of the quality of the coming harvest. The town also has a number of stone baronial houses, the ruins of a castle and possibly the oldest dwelling house in the region – although there is some dispute about this!

CALAHORRA (Rioja Baja) is a good base for visiting the more mountainous Baja area. It was originally a Roman town (*Calagurris*) and is the largest town in the Rioja Baja and one of the oldest – it celebrated its bi-millennium in 1982. It was the birthplace of the Roman orator Quintiliano in 35AD and the prolific Latin Christian writer and poet Aurelio Prudencio Clemente in 348AD. In 1045 it was re-conquered from the Moors and the massive town walls signify its strategic importance through the ages.

Calahorra is an interesting town with a Gothic church complete with flying buttresses, a neo-classical façade and an 18th century tower, and an interesting museum of paintings and sculptures. Do not miss the imposing ornamental baroque cathedral, a national monument containing three stunning altarpieces, and the baroque church. The colourful market, established in 1255 and still held on Thursdays, is also worth a visit. To complete your visit, you may wish to stay at the *Parador de Calahorra*, where those aged over 60 can take advantage of a 35 per cent discount (not applicable from July to September inclusive).

CAÑAS (Rioja Alta) is the site of the *Santa María* convent, begun in the 12th century, where the original exquisite windows can still be admired. Inside is the tomb of the Abbess Urraca

Lépez and an 18th century crib. The nuns still paint pottery and make beautiful embroidery to sell to visitors.

CASTLES. There are a number of Roman, Arabic and Medieval castles in Rioja including the *Castle of Davalillo* near San Asensio and substantial remains at Arnedo and Quel. The imposing and faithfully restored *Aguas Muertas Castle* at Agoncillo and the *Clavijo Rock* both have impressive walls and battlements, where fierce battles took place between the Moors and Christians in the 11th century. *Cuzcurrita de Río Tirón* castle dates from the 13th century and there is also a Gothic castle at Leiva. Somewhat surprisingly, the apartments in the well-preserved castle towers at Torremontalbo at Mahave are still inhabited.

CENICERO (Rioja Alta), to the west of Logroño on the River Ebro, was originally a Roman wine town and the burial place of the Roman legions stationed in the area (the name means 'ashtray' or 'ash bin' in Spanish). Each September an interesting wine festival is held in the large covered *pelota* (a Basque ball game) court, involving ten days of eating and drinking to celebrate the Patron Saint of *Santa Daria*, and culminating in the ritual pressing of the first wine of the year. This fortified town was originally built to protect against attacks by the Navarrans from across the river. Today's visitors can enjoy tranquil walks along the river banks or buy bread, paté and a bottle of wine and enjoy a picnic in the shade of the local woods and orchards, followed by a *siesta* – bliss!

CIDACOS VALLEY (Rioja Baja) was once the home of roaming dinosaurs, where you can still see dinosaur footprints (unfortunately for dinosaur hunters, made a few million years ago). The villages of Munilla and Enciso are of greatest interest, with marked trails and local guides to show you around. A booklet in English and a *Ruta de los Dinosaurios* (dinosaurs' route) leaflet are available from tourist offices.

ELCIEGO (Rioja Alavesa) is a hill village in the Basque Country facing Cenicero across the River Ebro. It is home of the ***Bodegas Marqués de Riscal***, founded in 1860, and ***Bodegas Valdelana*** established 17 years later. Elciego is noted for its steep, narrow streets and noble houses, complete with ancient crests (*escudos*), and a church with wonderful views of the local vineyards.

FUENMAYOR (Rioja Alta) is situated on the main N232 road between Haro and Logroño. It is an important wine town – rumour has it that even the mortar in the church was blended with wine – with impressive mansions decorated with coats of arms. There are nine bodegas in Fuenmayor, which, together with Cenicero, is second in importance to Haro in the hierarchy of Rioja Alta wine production.

HORMILLEJA (Rioja Alta) is a small village situated in the midst of vineyards, where the majority of the area's Garnacha grapes are grown.

LABASTIDA (Rioja Alavesa), north-east of Haro in the Basque Country was originally a walled frontier town established in the 8th century, and is situated on the side of Mount Toloño with striking views over the River Ebro valley. It is historically important as the birthplace of *M. Quintano*, who introduced the wine-ageing techniques in Rioja in the 18th century. Calle Mayor (most towns with a medieval quarter have a main street named Calle Mayor) contains palatial mansions with ornately-cut eaves. The *Shrine of Santa María de la Piscina* was formerly a military fortress and the town hall a Renaissance palace, while the *Church of the Asunción* has an impressive ornamental altarpiece and one of the most prized organs in the region.

There are five bodegas in Labastida, where **Remelluri** is housed in late medieval ruins originally owned by the Monastery of Toloño containing an 11th century necropolis and 13th century *ermita* (hermitage). There is also an interesting museum that can be visited daily except Sundays. Labastida is also the home of one of the best co-operatives in Rioja, *Unión de Cosecheros de Labastida*.

LAGUARDIA (Rioja Alavesa) began life as a castle (founded on a town called *Biazteri*) built on a hill in the Basque Country to repel the Moors. It is a picturesque and atmospheric walled town riddled with a maze of underground cellars, which played an important role when the Moors besieged it. The inhabitants not only continued to live safely underground, but with their secret entrances and exits in the hillside, could replenish their supplies at will. The town (pop. 1,200), the capital of the Rioja Alavesa and an important wine centre, is a distinctive landmark that can be seen for miles around. Spanish tourists flock there, mainly at weekends, so a weekday trip makes it easier to wander around the narrow streets and visit the local bodegas. You can admire the tiny houses through their inviting open doors and see the ancient cobbled rooms that were once stables for horses used not only for working the fields but also to defend the town against attacks.

Detailed local information is available from the friendly tourist office (English is spoken), who, for a few pesetas, can arrange a visit to the ornate *Church of Santa María de los Reyes* to view the impressive wooden frescos. The 16th century Gothic façade, protected from the ravages of time by a Renaissance façade built over it, contains carved figures inside, which remain beautifully alive and bright even today. Laguardia has another exquisite church, the gothic *Church of San Juan Bautista*, which has an impressive organ.

The town's access gates, protective walls and many stately homes dating from the 16th to 18th centuries remain intact in their original medieval layout – at night when lights are shining from the numerous windows the effect is absolutely magical. The *Torre Abacial* was originally built as a military look-out tower, although during the numerous alterations over the years the battlements have been removed. In the old town is the 14th century *Casa de la Primicia* in Calle de Paganos, reportedly the oldest conserved building.

The *Casa del Vino* in Laguardia is the centre for the study of Alavesa wines and houses interesting exhibits on viticulture and oenology, as well as local history. The centre includes modern wine laboratories and advises the local smaller wine producers (*cosecheros*) on wine related problems and also on ways of producing and marketing their wines, instead of selling wines and grapes in bulk.

The small *Marixa* hotel in Laguardia is recommended and has a number of rooms with lovely views over the surrounding countryside. It also boasts an excellent restaurant stocked with a vast selection of wines and suitably large *copas* so you can swirl your wine with gusto. Also in Laguardia is the *Hotel Castillo el Collado*, a distinctive hotel of immense character, which has been lovingly restored by the owner, Javier Acillona. The Tower Room, suggestively called *Amor y Locura* (Love & Madness), is the ideal place for a romantic break, which, together with Javier's wonderful cooking and superb Riojas, will ensure a memorable stay. If you are seeking something lighter, try the *Errjoxako Batzokja Bar* in Mayor de Migueloa, where Sandy (an American) produces some of the most delicious *tortillas* in the whole of Spain – delicioso! Husband José is a wealth of knowledge about Laguardia and Riojan wines – all (including José junior) speak English and will make you very welcome.

LA HOYA (Rioja Alavesa), discovered in 1935 just outside Laguardia, is a pre-historic settlement dating back to 1500BC. It is believed to have been founded by a tribe from the north who were then assimilated into the community which had inhabited the area for several millenniums. The small museum on the site explains the history of this important find.

NAJERA (Rioja Alta) is a picturesque town west of Logroño, situated on the hilly southern edge of the Rioja Alta. Once the capital of Rioja, the Kings of Navarra had a residence here and the 11th century monastery of *Santa María la Real* contains many tombs of the Kings and Queens of Navarra, Castile and Leon. Even the mysterious plants grown for their liqueur didn't guarantee immortality! Navarra's first coinage was also struck in Najera.

NAVARRETE   (Rioja Alta) is a hill town south west of Logroño with impressive baronial houses and a fine 16th century church decorated with Flemish triptych and goldsmith's work. Henry of Trastamara was defeated here by Peter the Cruel and the Black Prince in 1367.

OLLAURI   (Rioja Alta), just south of Haro, is a small village and one of the most beautiful in the area. It has outstanding two-storey mansions adorned with noble heraldic shields, elegant façades and large picture windows. Wander through the fascinating streets to the parish church and admire the resplendent baroque altarpiece. The village also contains numerous underground cellars, both in the houses and the bodegas. Do not miss the ventilation shafts dating from the Middle Ages, which sprout like mushrooms on the slopes above the village and were built to maintain a constant humidity and temperature in the wine cellars below. Nearby is *Bodegas Beronia*, which sits in a attractive natural setting surrounded by vineyards, and **Bodegas Marqués de Griñón**, with its 200-year-old cellars and a museum.

OYON (or Oión, Rioja Alavesa) is a small town across the river from Logroño in the Basque Country. It was an important stopping point on the *Pilgrims' Way*, where the 17th century *Church de la Asunción* is noted for its extremely ornate tower. Oyón is the home of **Bodegas El Coto, Faustino Martínez, Marqués de Vitoria** and **Bodegas Martínez Bujanda**, the latter with a fine museum containing tools and presses over 100 years old. The road to Laguardia from Oyón winds through an impressive landscape of vineyards – if you time your visit for early November, the dramatic variation in colour of the dying leaves on the vines is truly breathtaking – the Rioja equivalent of the fall in America's New England.

SANTA DOMINGO de la CALZADA is situated south of Haro and just outside the official Rioja wine area. It is on the old *Pilgrims' Route* to Santiago de Compostela and was founded by Santo Domingo, who erected a causeway in the 11th century over the River Oja for pilgrims to cross. High on a wall of the 12th century Romanesque-Byzantine cathedral, behind a grill, are a live cock and hen, commemorating a miracle wrought by San Dominic, the Patron Saint of pilgrims. Although miracles by their very nature are unusual occurrences, this one bears repeating!

A young and pure pilgrim passing through the town resisted, no doubt with great difficulty, the amorous advances of the innkeeper's rather sexy daughter, who, unaccustomed to being spurned, falsely accused him of theft. The unfortunate young man was hanged, but through the miraculous intervention of the Saint, he did not die. The local judge, interrupted while dining on a pair of roast chickens, was told of this and understandably retorted that this must be nonsense and that the pilgrim was as dead as the chickens on his table – when lo and behold! – the birds sprouted feathers, stood up, crowed and promptly flew out of the window! The wronged pilgrim was cut down and continued on his way to Santiago and hopefully lived happily ever after.

There is a *parador* (luxury hotel) next to the cathedral housed in a 12th century hospice, which sheltered pilgrims on the road to Santiago. Its impressive lobby features Gothic arches, stone pillars and a wooden moulded ceiling, while the restaurant offers local specialities and Riojan wines.

SAN MILLAN de la COGOLLA (Rioja Alta) is the site of two monasteries, *Suso* and *Yuso*, situated in a stunningly beautiful and peaceful area, 15km (9mi) from Najera and Santo Domingo de la Calzada, next to the Valdezcaray ski resort. The *Suso* monastery, high in the mountains, dates from the 10th century and was originally built to guard the cave where a holy hermit lived in reclusion. The *Yuso* monastery, built between the 15th and 17th centuries, is known as *The Riojan Escorial* (after the enormous palace in Madrid). Yuso is further down the valley and much bigger and more impressive than Suso, with a dazzling interior, one wing of which is now a luxury modern hotel and restaurant. A visit is both a visual feast and a spiritual experience, and the Abbey Church contains many treasures, including the remains of San Millán in a massive tomb complete with ivory ornamentation. Historically the Yuso monastery is extremely important, as the oldest known documents written in the Spanish and Basque languages were found in its libraries.

SAN VICENTE de la SONSIERRA   (Rioja Alta) is a picturesque village dominated by a ruined castle and church on the top of a hill, reached by walking or driving through the extremely narrow streets, constantly worrying whether there is sufficient room for your car! However, the magnificent views across the vineyards of Rioja, the River Ebro with its medieval and more recent new bridges, and the backdrop of the Sierra de la Demanda and Sierra de Cantabria mountains, make the effort well worthwhile. Standing on top of this hill you will fully appreciate why the church tower is a wind-foiling, asymmetric design!

In the town is the 12th century Church of *Santa María de la Piscina*, a Romanesque mansion, a necropolis, and nearby, the *Dolmen de la Cascaja*. At Easter, during the festival of *Los Picados*, hooded penitents with long pointed hats walk in procession through the village flagellating themselves with 5kg (11lb) whips – the resulting blisters are then pricked by members of the local *Brotherhood of La Vera Cruz de los Disciplantes*! This practice, once common in other countries, is for some reason, the last remaining one in Europe. Hopefully the penitents are fortified with the local wine!

VILLABUENA de ALAVA (Rioja Alavesa) is a true wine village with no less than 32 bodegas and numerous noblemen's houses. It is advisable to walk around the narrow, hilly streets to visit the numerous bodegas and view the *Church of San Andrés* and the *Shrine of Santa María*.

Architectural Glossary

Altarpiece: A sculpture or painting (or combination) covering the wall behind the altar, which may be made of wood, stone or metal and bear religious scenes.

Baroque: The artistic style of the late 16th to early 18th centuries, characterised by dynamism, sensuality and the extreme ornamentation of its forms and lines.

Coffered: An ornamental sunken panel in a ceiling or dome.

Dolmen: A funeral construction from the Bronze Age, 2650 to 900BC, comprising large superimposed stone slabs normally covered with earth and stone.

Gothic: A European architectural style from the 12th to 16th centuries, characterised by the verticality and levity of its structures, the lancet arch, the ribbed vault and flying buttress.

Herreran style: Named after the architect Juan de Herrera, who designed in the austere style decreed by King Philip II in the 16th century.

Neo-Classical: Late 18th and early 19th century artistic style based on surviving classical models of Greco-Roman art – a reaction to the baroque and rococo styles.

Necropolis: An ancient burial ground.

Plateresque: Early Renaissance architecture, characterised by a profusion of decorative details reminiscent of silver filigree. Plateresque literally means 'silversmith-like'.

Renaissance: A cultural movement from the 15th and 16th centuries characterised by the revival of culture and art from classical antiquity.

Romanesque: An artistic style from the 9th to 13th centuries, characterised by massive masonry wall construction with barrel vaults, rounded arches and few openings or windows.

Festivals

The Riojanos love festivals and all villages and towns celebrate their Patron Saint's day, filling the bars and streets with their noisy exuberance until the early hours of the morning. In addition to Riojan wines, revellers are fuelled by *zurracapote,* a seductive blend of wine, brandy, fruit and cinnamon, prepared by wine-makers and served free to allcomers.

Visit and join in the fun – be prepared to be chased by bulls in the streets of **Alfaro** (Rioja Baja) from August 15th to 18th, to be sprayed with red wine in **Haro** on June 29th, deluged in rosé wine in **San Asensio** on 25th July, witness ritual flogging in **San Vicente de la Sonsierra** at Easter, dance on stilts (!) at **Anguiano** on 22nd July, be showered with bread, fish and wine in **Logroño** on June 11th, be choked with aromatic smoke in **Arnedillo** on 30th November, and covered in multi-coloured smoke in the nearby village of **Peroblasco** on the last Saturday in July.

You can also try to 'Rob the Saints' in **Arnedo** on the 27th September, tread grapes in **Logroño** on 21st September, or be enchanted by the *son et lumière* in the Knights' Cloister at the *Monastery of Santa María la Real* in **Nájera** during the second fortnight of July. Also to be enjoyed are the many colourful processions including **Santa Domingo de la Calzada** in May, **Calahorra** (March and August), and the equally colourful dances staged in **Briones** in September and **Nieva** on the 25th and 26th July. *The Feria de San Mateo* in **Logroño** on 21st September, which once marked the beginning of the *vendimia,* is a religious festival but with plenty of joyous drinking.

South of Logroño in the **River Iregua Valley**, processions, dances and general festivities take place throughout the year, many celebrating ancient legends and traditions. In the **Cidacos Valley** at **Quel**, you may be pelted with bread and cheese from the hermitage's windows, complete with accompanying wine.

La Battala dos Viños (the battle of wines) takes place on San Pedro's day (29th June) in **Haro**, when over 4,000 join in this exuberant three-hour battle. It commemorates a 10th century property dispute between Haro and the neighbouring town of Miranda, although the wine battle started only in 1906 (no one knows how or why). Wine is traditionally 'fired' from *botas* (flasks made from hide), which although very accurate cannot compete with modern fire extinguishers that fire half a bottle of wine in five seconds! Some 50,000 litres of wine are sprayed in three hours, with the local council providing four litres per person. No one is spared, so wear old clothes and carry a waterproof camera!

Logroño's festivities are joyous affairs celebrating all manner of events, with *mucho* drinking, colourful processions, grape treading and bullfights. The *Festival of San Bernabé* is held on the 11th June in memory of a siege by French troops during the reign of Carlos I in 1521, when thanks are given to the Saint for his protection. Everyone who goes to the Revellín Gate on this date is traditionally given fish, bread and wine by the *Fish Brotherhood*. A procession is held, with the Mayor of Logroño waving the city flag to signify its possession.

The *Feria de San Mateo* dates back 900 years and is held on St Matthew's Day, September 21st, in Logroño's main square, the Espolón. It lasts for a week and marks the start of the wine harvest (*vendimia*), commencing with grape treading and an offering of the first grape juice to the *Patron of La Rioja*, followed by a procession of floats whose displays vividly portray the importance of wine to the region. The exuberant marching bands, bullfights and dramatic midnight firework displays – not to mention the free-flowing *vino* – ensure that the festivities are a spectacular celebration.

There is no shortage of ways to enjoy yourself with friendly Riojans and their wonderful zest for life, encouraging you to join in. You will be made really welcome, sometimes literally with open arms!

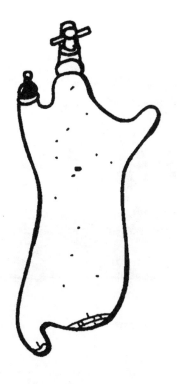

El Puente de Cihuri

4.

WINE ROUTES

This chapter includes five suggested wine routes, visiting all three of Riojan wine sub-regions: the Rioja Alavesa, the Rioja Alta and the Rioja Baja. Also included are a bodega and monastery route, and the section of the *Pilgrims' Way to Santiago de Compostela* as it wends its way through La Rioja. Each route includes details of places of interest in addition to bodegas to visit along the way. In the majority of cases, visits, which invariably include tastings, are by appointment only (telephone and/or fax numbers, visiting hours and languages spoken are detailed in **Chapter 2**). All routes can be studied and planned using Michelin map number 442 (*España Norte*) or the Geo Planeta map of La Rioja (1:250,000).

Both Haro and Logroño, the starting and finishing points for some routes, contain a wealth of bodegas which are listed in **Chapter 3** (Visiting Rioja).

Route 1 – Haro to Baños de Ebro (ca. 45km/28mi)

We start our journey in Haro (see page 98), taking the LR202 for Sajazarra, crossing over the A68 *autovía* and Río Oja to Anguciano. Here you will find the *Castillo Torre fuerte de los Salcedo*, a 14th century fortified tower and private residence. Continue to Sajazarra (which hosts a music festival in August)

to *Bodegas Señorío de Líbano* (English and French spoken) housed in a 15th century medieval castle. The town boasts another 15th century *castillo* and the ornate church of *Virgen de la Antigua*. Heading out of Sajazarra, take the LR301 for Cuzcurrita, which has a 15th century castle and the Romanesque *Shrine of Sorejan*, together with two bodegas. *Castillo de Cuzcurrita* was originally a 14th century castle and is the family's home, with gardens surrounded by the vineyard. *Benito Urbina* was founded in the 19th century and has old stone cellars and oak vats (English and French are spoken).

Leaving Cuzcurrita take the LR201 to **Tirgo**, where you will find **Bodegas Castresana** (visits daily by appointment), and continue on to **Casalarreina** and **Bodegas Ajuarte** (French spoken). Leaving Casalarreina on the N232, pass beneath the A68 and head to **Ollauri**, one of the most beautiful villages in the area with elegant two-storey mansions adorned with striking façades and noble heraldic shields. Also worth visiting are the stone parish church with its splendid baroque altarpiece and the medieval, cellar ventilation shafts sprouting from the slopes above the village. The high quality local grapes are used by the two important bodegas here, **Bodega Beronia**, a traditional bodega situated in a lovely natural setting surrounded by vineyards (English and French spoken), and *Marqués de Griñón*, which although founded only in 1994 was built in typical Riojan bodega style and used the existing 200-year-old cellars. They also have a museum.

Leave Ollauri on the N232 and after 4km you will arrive at **Briones**, a walled village of great historical and artistic interest. The buildings are predominantly stone, although wood and brick are also used, and include one of the oldest in Rioja. Several buildings in the town square have carvings of dogs in their eaves and there are a number of interesting churches in the centre including the octagonal, 18th century baroque *Santo Cristo de los Remedios* and the exquisite parish church of *Santa María*. This has three naves and was begun in the 16th century and enlarged in the 18th century by the same stonemasons who built the twin towers of *La Redondo* in Logroño. Inside is a Gothic statue of Christ and various fine examples of Riojan baroque on the altarpieces and a superb baroque organ still used for concerts today. To appreciate the town's fine setting and defensive position, take a stroll around the town walls and admire the panoramic views of the Rioja Alta and La Sonsierra beneath the Herrera and Peñacerrado peaks.

Continuing on the N232, our next stop is **San Asensio**, between the Ebro and Najerilla rivers, a typical Rioja Alta town in both its design and the sandstone construction of its buildings. All are adorned with heraldic shields, eaves, ironwork and stone corner pieces, and some also have balcony and window lintels. The town square contains some outstanding arcades, while the stone parish church incorporates old Romanesque materials and a neo-classical altarpiece.

San Asensio is famous for its rosé wine and stages an annual *Rosé Wine Battle* on 25th July when wine is liberally showered on everyone in sight – take a waterproof camera and definitely do not wear your best clothes! One of the area's most notable folklore displays is held just outside the village during the San Asensio dances, which are part of the festivities in honour of the Patron Saint.

There are four bodegas in San Asensio including *Vinícola Davalillo Coop*, situated next to the Monastery of La Estrella with beautiful views of the River Ebro and the 12th century castles of Davalillo and Vicente. The others are *Bodegas Afersa* and *Bodegas Perica*, the latter housed in an extremely old original building, and *El Arca de Noé Coop*, where visitors require no appointments (open daily except Sunday from 9am to 1.30pm and 3 to 7.30pm).

Leaving San Asensio, take the N232 to **Torremontalbo** and the River Najerilla, where the Rioja Alta becomes much greener due to the abundant poplar groves. Torremontalbo is a riverside village dating from the 11th century with a privately-owned *torre fuerte* (fortified tower) from the 14th to 15th centuries with lovely gardens (unfortunately not open to visitors). *Bodegas Amézola de la Mora*, built in cut-stone, has cellars well over 100 years old and is attractively surrounded by vineyards (French is spoken).

We now leave the Rioja Alta and enter the Rioja Alavesa at **Baños de Ebro**, an old Roman settlement, where the *Shrine of la Santa Cruz* is found. Here *Bodegas Varal* is surrounded by vineyards and has attractive views over the countryside, while the modern bodegas of *García Chávarri* and *Berzal Otero* (English spoken) are situated in the town.

It is now possible to continue with wine route 2 to **Villabuena** or return to Haro.

Route 2 – Villabuena to Briñas (30km/19mi)

Wine Routes 1 & 2 can be combined to make a round tour by continuing on from Baños de Ebro to Villabuena, rather than returning to Haro.

Continuing from Baños de Ebro (Route 1) on the N232 you will come to **Villabuena**, which is home to no less than 32 bodegas, the largest number in a single town in Rioja. At the southern end of the village there is a detailed map to help you negotiate the narrow streets. After parking your car your first stop should be the *Church of San Andrés* and the *Shrine of Santa María*. There are two bodegas in Villabuena that can be visited without appointments, *Berrueco Pérez* (daily from 10am to 2pm and 4 to 8pm), a traditional Alavesa bodega with cellars cut from solid rock and an old press on display, and *García Berrueco*. *Bodegas Luis Cañas* is an old bodega with spectacular views (English spoken), while *Biagorri Anguiano* was founded at the turn of the century. It is housed in a new building constructed in 1980 and (uniquely) uses storage tanks coated in epoxy resin for optimum preservation of the wines.

Pérez Maestresala is modern but with old-style, vaulted cellars, while *Salázar Rodrigo* is a 1905 bodega hewn from solid rock and dubbed the 'bodega of the priests' due to its earlier connection with collecting clerical tithes. *Viñedos y Bodegas de la Marquesa, SMS* was founded in 1880 and is a stone bodega with underground cellars hewn from solid rock. *Viña Villabuena* is a large bodega containing 5,000 oak barrels, which also has an air-conditioned hotel.

Leave Villabuena on the narrow twisty road (A3214) to **Samaniego**. In the village is the *Church of the Asunción*, formerly an ancient fortress, and three interesting bodegas well worth visiting (appointments are necessary). *Bodegas Ostatu* was founded in 1720 and is a listed neo-classical palace, formerly an inn, with a sensitively designed extension. *Bodegas Virgen del Valle* was founded only in 1987 but, nevertheless, boasts 17th century cellars hewn from solid rock. The third bodega is *Pascual Larrieta*, founded in 1790 (and recently modernised), with an 18th century, underground vaulted cellar containing an antique two-screw manual press.

Leave Samaniego, and before heading west to Abalos on the A124, turn right towards Laguardia (Biasteri in Basque) and near the hospital take the mountain road (A2124) to Vitoria (Gasteiz). This 4km (2.5mi) diversion will take you to the **Balcón de la Rioja** at the imposing Herrera mountain pass, with its stunning views over the surrounding countryside. Although a spectacular picnic area complete with fresh mountain water gurgling from an underground stream, it is rather prone to plagues of flies in hot weather, but the views are truly impressive.

Next drive downhill to the A124 and turn right towards the interesting village of **Abalos**, with its narrow streets (it is advisable to park your car and walk) and stone 17th and 18th century buildings, many embossed with their original owners' coats of arms. Here you will find the *Palace of the Marqués de Legarda*, the ornate 16th century *Church of San Estéban*, containing a priceless 16th century altarpiece, and the single nave Romanesque *Shrine of San Felices*, recently restored. On the edge of the village, carved into rocks, are 10th century tombs and fascinating grape-treading indentations. There are seven bodegas, with English spoken at two: ***Garrido García***, who will also organise a tour of the village church, local mansions and religious and lay art, and ***Bodega de la Real Divisa***, one of the oldest bodegas in Europe dating from the 12th century. Visits are possible daily, although they prefer weekends (English and French are spoken).

Bodegas Solana de Ramírez Ruíz is built in the style of a castle in the centre of town, surrounded by old houses and trees, with a nearby museum of traditional viticultural and vinicultural artefacts. ***Puelles Fernández*** is on the west side of the village – rather than walk it is better to return to your car and drive carefully through the narrow streets. It is situated in a picturesque setting overlooking the countryside and mountains. Jesús will show you around the bodega and, if you make an appointment for 4.30pm, also his water-mill.

Return through Abalos and turn right on to the A124 road and head for **San Vicente de la Sonsierra**, where there are seven bodegas, one of which, ***Bodegas Valgrande***, does not require visitors to make an appointment (English and French are spoken). In San Vicente there are a number of interesting sights including the 12th century *Church of Santa María de la Piscina*, a Romanesque mansion, a necropolis and the nearby *Dolmen of la Cascaja*. It is worth driving or walking through the narrow streets to the fortified church at the top of the hill, from where there are magnificent panoramic views. These include both the Cantabria and Demanda mountain ranges, the River Ebro with its picturesque medieval bridge (flanked by a modern one) and vineyards stretching as far as the eye can see.

At Easter the festival of *Los Picados* is not to be missed, although it is not for the squeamish (see page). ***Bodegas Señorío de San Vicente*** (English and French are spoken), although founded only in 1991, has a fully restored 150-year-old building containing 15,000 litre wooden vats. ***Bodegas Sierra Cantabria*** (founded in 1954) is built in contemporary style incorporating 300-year-old stone in the building and is one of the leaders in the production of young, *joven*, wines (French is spoken). ***Bodegas Hermanos Peciña*** is a recent bodega (established 1997) with wood-ageing facilities and where English is spoken, as it is at **Bodegas Sonsierra Coop**. **Bodegas Ramírez** was also recently established (1987), although the old bodega built in 1927 is still in existence here. They combine traditional and modern methods, producing wines by carbonic maceration (French is spoken).

We now head out of the Rioja Alta on the LR132 and arrive in the Rioja Alavesa at **Labastida**, originally a walled frontier town on the side of Mount Toloño overlooking the Ebro valley. The *Shrine of Santa María de la Piscina* was formerly a military fortress and the town hall a Renaissance palace. Labastida is famous as the birthplace of *M. Quintano*, who introduced Rioja's wine-ageing techniques in the 18th century.

There are five bodegas here, of which only the welcoming **Remelluri** (just outside the village at Rivas de Tereso) speak English. The Bodega was founded in 1967 and is housed in late medieval ruins, with the main building dating from the 18th century. The original farm was owned by the monastery of Toloño and the beautiful estate includes an 11th century necropolis and a 13th century shrine. They also have small but interesting museum open daily (except Sundays) from 8am to noon and 3 to 5pm. **Bodegas Gil García, Santiago** (visits daily by appointment) have a 16th century cave hewn out of solid rock and a stone fermentation pool, while **Quintana, Quintana Ponciano** have 250-year-old cellars and use only their own grapes.

Finally on to **Briñas**, a large village of great historic and artistic importance, home to more mansions than any town in the region. The impressive 16th century parish *Church of the Asunción* in the old Plaza de la Constitución has a beautiful 17th century altarpiece, while nearby there is a wall fountain with vaulted pipes from the 12th century and a cross dated 1569 rising above the wine cellars' ventilation shafts. Briñas has a medieval bridge over the River Ebro and is known as both the wine cellar village and Rioja's 'door and balcony'. **Bodegas Ayala Lete e Hijos** is over 100 years old and has a 440m² (4,736ft²) underground cellar of cut stone (visits daily except Sunday), while just outside Briñas is **Bodegas Eduardo Domínguez Fernández**. If you are looking for somewhere special to rest your head, the excellent *Hospedería Señorío de*

Briñas hotel has very friendly hosts and is highly recommended.

Leaving the village towards Haro, you pass by the interesting *Portal de la Rioja* wine museum, situated on the corner of the N124 to Vitoria (it also sells a wide selection of wines). They are open daily (except Mondays) from 10am to 2pm and from 4 to 8pm. Briñas is just 3km from Haro, where Route 2 terminates.

Route 3 – Logroño to Fuenmayor (30km/19mi)

Although concentrated within a small area, Route 3 takes in all three of Rioja's wine sub-regions. Starting at Logroño (see page 102), head for **Viana** (on the N111 to Pamplona), which although within the Rioja Baja wine area, is actually situated in the province of Navarra. In Viana you will find *Bodega Ondarre*, a unique and striking modern building in stone with Arabic tiles. This bodega is unusual as it also makes Cava sparkling wine (visits weekdays – English is spoken).

Leaving the village on the A4210 towards Moreda de Alaya, turn off onto the A3226 to **Oyón** (Oion) in the Rioja Alavesa, where the 17th century *Church de la Asunción* has a splendid ornate tower. There are four bodegas in Oyón, all of which require visitors to make appointments – **Bodegas Faustino**, founded in 1861 and famous for their frosted, antique-looking bottles, request two weeks notice (English, French and German are spoken). Another old firm is **Bodegas Martínez Bujanda** (founded in 1889), which has a wine museum containing tools and presses over 100 years old (English, French and German also spoken). **Marqués de Vitoria** is housed in a rustic building with a wooden porch and a beautiful barrel-ageing area with a wooden ceiling and oak beams. They make wine with ecologically grown grapes (French is spoken). **El Coto de Rioja** restricts visits to Mondays to Thursdays (English is spoken).

Our next stop (on the A2126) is the interesting village of **Yécora**, boasting a 12th century fountain, a 13th century shrine, and a 16th century church. **Bodegas Coop San Sixto** and **Jalón López** arrange daily visits and conducted tours of the village, but only Spanish is spoken. At **Laserna**, in the Rioja Alavesa, there is an old Roman bridge over the river Ebro with just two arches remaining. Here **Viñedos del Contino** occupies a 16th century house now containing new cellars holding 1,650 oak barrels, surrounded by vineyards (English is spoken). Still in the Rioja Alavesa, we arrive next at the village of **Assa**, where **Urarte Espinosa** (founded in 1290!) still use the caves originally excavated in 1286 (visits daily by appointment). The bodega has a 1,000-year-old oak tree, a paddock, a snack-bar and lovely riverside walks – and they also stage bullfights!

We now move on to **Lapuebla de Labarca**, where there is the 16th century *Church of La Asunción* with its uneven towers and arched portal with five segmented balconies. There are eight bodegas here, at three of which English, French and/or German are spoken. **Casado Manzanos** bodega (visits daily) was built in 1942 in stone with an Arabic tiled roof and concrete fermentation pools and tanks (now also stainless steel). **Casada Fuertes, Herminio** has ancient eight metre deep cellars (daily visits), while **Zugober** (founded in 1988) have stainless steel facilities and weekday visits between 9am and 2pm. At **Aguirre Viteri** you can see 5,500-litre wooden vats over 150 years old, while the old bodega of **Casado Fuertes, Luis** has oak barrels and vats, and concrete fermentation pools (both have daily visits).

Leaving Lapuebla de Labarca (and Rioja Alavesa) on the LR251, we come to **Fuenmayor** in the Rioja Alta, one of the region's major wine centres with mansions and noble houses decorated with impressive coats-of-arms. Here English is spoken at six of the seven bodegas, but unfortunately they all require appointments to be made in advance.

Bodegas A.G.E. have several buildings dating from 1881 (visits daily except Sunday), while **Bodegas Cardema** was founded only in 1993 (visits daily, English and French spoken) and the functional and modern **Bodegas Lan** (weekday visits, English spoken) in 1970. **Bodegas Vallemayor,** founded in 1985, has almost 1,000 barrels (English and French spoken), while **Bodegas Montecillo** is a striking 19th century bodega cut from solid rock with distinctive niches for the ageing of its *gran reservas*. English and French are spoken.

Bodegas Marqués del Puerto (founded in 1972) is a lovely bodega situated between Fuenmayor and Logroño, with an elegant spiral staircase leading down to the ageing cellars containing 4,200 oak barrels. Weekday visits, except August, when they are closed (English and French are spoken). **Propiedad Grial** is built in contemporary style and surrounded by vineyards (visits daily by appointment and English is spoken). **Unión de Viticultores Riojanos** have an elegant cut stone building and welcome visitors daily (English, French and German are spoken).

Although this ends **Wine Route 3**, you may continue with **Wine Route 4** (below), which commences at **Cenicero** that is 9km (6mi) from Fuenmayor on the N232.

Route 4 – Cenicero to Elvillar (25km/15mi)

Wine Routes 3 & 4 can be combined to make a round tour by continuing on from Fuenmayor to Cenicero, rather than returning to Logroño.

This tour begins at **Cenicero** in the Rioja Alta, a famous wine town, 24km (15mi) from Haro on the N232 and also reachable via the A68 Motorway (1km from Junction 9). Cenicero lies at the junction of two rivers, the Ebro and Najerilla, where there is a bridge over the ravine, and is a pre-Roman town with various sites remaining from that period. In the past there were frequent clashes with the Navarrans from across the river and Cenicero was originally a fortified town (there are the remains of a fortified house in the village).

Many of the town's old stone houses were built as three storey, four-part houses with underground wine cellars, and in the old town the original Gothic windows have been re-used and the traditional decorative shields retained. The parish *Church of San Martin* is built of stone in typical Riojan baroque style. This interesting town also has a number of striking sculptures depicting the harvest and working tractors, although the most notable and surprising is a copy of the Statue of Liberty, erected in memory of the town's defenders who opposed the Carlists in 1834.

In the first week of September you can forget about visiting bodegas – there are ten days of eating, drinking and partying, culminating in the ritual pressing of the first wine of the year on the final day. As a pleasant diversion from the merry-making you can take a peaceful stroll along the riverbank or in the surrounding woods and orchards.

Of the five bodegas in Cenicero, English is spoken (as well as French and German) only at *Bodegas Riojanas*, which produces excellent wines. They are to be found on the main road near the railway line, built by the French in 1890. The bodega was also founded in 1890 and is housed in a 19th century, Bordeaux Château-style building with gates (leading to the vineyards) dating from 1799. Weekday visits are at 11am.

Bodegas Berberana was founded in 1877 and has 40,000m² (430,000ft²) of grandiose buildings constructed in 1971 (visits by appointment). *Real Compañia de Viños* was established in 1949, although the wood and stone, beamed building was built in the mid-1800s. It was previously owned by Benedictine Monks who distilled liqueurs there until it was then converted into a bodega (the restoration was completed only in 1988). Visits by appointment between 9am and 5pm. *The Bod. Coop Santa Daría* have stainless steel facilities and weekday visits (French spoken), while *Pérez Artacho* have traditional vinification of their own harvest (visits daily from 9am to 8pm).

Leaving the Rioja Alta on the A3210, we now return to the Rioja Alavesa and travel to **Elciego**, a small but important wine village. The *Church of San Andrés* was designed by the same architect as the 16th century *Church of la Asunción* in Lapuebla, and has similar uneven towers (maybe the artisans were fortified with too much wine). It also has an arched portal with a gallery and seven balconies – an increase over the five of Lapuebla – a sign of local one-upmanship perhaps!

It is home to nine bodegas where English and French are mostly spoken (visits by appointment). *Marqués de Riscal* dates back to 1860 and is built of stone in the French Médoc style. It is the oldest bodega in the *Denominación* and the first to introduce the Bordeaux vinification style to Rioja. Visits are by appointment mornings and afternoons (closed noon to 2.30pm) from September to June, July from 8am to 2pm only and closed in August. Nearly as old (founded in 1877) is *Bodegas Valdelana*, where the stone cellars and façade were built in the late 19th century. They still press their grapes by foot, believing this to be the best method, as do many producers in other wine regions. Valdelana have a small but interesting museum and can be visited from 8am to 9pm on weekdays and 8am to 3pm at weekends.

The classic *Bodega Murúa* has ancient origins, although formed only in 1964, and is attractively enclosed by vineyards. It has a library dedicated to historical and oenological subjects, which can be visited (along with the bodega) on weekday mornings and afternoons (closed from 1 to 3pm). *Palacios Sáez* originally belonged to the legendary Marqués de Legarda and has three cellars with stone arches dating back some 400 years and a cut-stone façade. Visits are daily between 9am and 9pm, except Sunday when they are afternoons only (French is spoken). There are restricted visits to *Bodegas Domecq* (when English is spoken) and weekday visits (closed lunchtimes) to the 1934 *Bodegas Muriel*. *Viña Paterna*, a 150-year-old mansion with attractive 17th century underground facilities (visits daily except Sunday, English and French spoken). *Viña Salceda* (English spoken), situated in the centre of a 15ha (37 acres) estate, can be visited on weekday mornings and afternoons (closed 1 to 3.30pm).

We now take the A3212 to **Navaridas** and *Guzmán Alonso*, an old bodega founded in 1900 and housed in a Renaissance house displaying a 17th century coat of arms. It was originally the country estate of Guzmán Aldazábal. Meals are served at the bodega and visits arranged daily with wine tastings complete with a commentary.

Backtracking to Elciego on the A3212, we take the narrow winding A3210 road through attractive countryside packed with vineyards to **Laguardia**, the capital of the Rioja Alavesa and one of the prettiest villages in Spain (complete with its resident nesting storks). The town commands a hilltop overlooking the Alavesa vineyards and is a fascinating, medieval fortified town that is a maze of narrow streets and alleyways. The town has long been an important military centre and is now the commercial heart of the Rioja Alavesa. The House of Wine (*Casa del Vino*) is an official Basque wine institute helping local winegrowers with courses in viticulture, oenology and other technical expertise. They also help with the investment and promotion of Alavesa wines (as distinct from other sub-regions of Rioja) and more specifically small individual wine producers.

There are ten bodegas in and around Laguardia, the oldest of which is **Santamaría Güénaga** dating back to 1300. This bodega originally belonged to Samaniego, the Spanish equivalent of Æsop, famous for his fables. English is spoken at five bodegas, all of which require appointments with the exception of **Bodegas Palacio** (founded in 1894), who schedule visits on the hour (weekdays, except Mondays, from 11am to 2pm and weekends noon to 2pm). They also have their own hotel.

English, French and German are spoken at **Bodegas Campillo** (founded in 1990). **Bodegas Casa Juan** is housed in an old flour mill containing a museum of Equatorial African Art (French is spoken). Although recently constructed, **Bodegas Luís Alegre** is of traditional style (it was founded in 1978 in a cave in Laguardia) and has maintained old traditions complemented with modern equipment (English and French are spoken). A baroque 17th century mansion with an underground cellar of the same age (1619) is home to **Bodegas Mayor de Migueloa**, which also has a hotel and restaurant (English and French are spoken). Both these languages are also spoken at **Cosecheros Alaveses** and **Santamaría López**, the latter of which has an impressive ageing cellar containing 1,500 American and French oak barrels.

Leaving Laguardia, turn left on to the N-232 (signposted Vitoria/Gasteiz) and after just 2km you arrive at **Páganos**, where, situated between two dolmens (*Sotillo* and *San Martín*), is **Bodegas Heredad de Ugarte** (English is spoken). The bodega has wonderful views of the Sierra de Cantabria mountains to the north and a balcony overlooking the pretty Rioja Alavesa vineyards in the south. Next we arrive at **Bodega Torre de Oña**, situated between Laguardia and Páganos on the ancient *Pilgrims' Way* (French is spoken). Finally, we end the tour at **Elvillar**, where the fortified church reputedly has the best 16th century altarpiece in the whole of the Rioja Alavesa. Elvillar has just one bodega, *García Viñegra*, founded in 1916 (visits by appointment).

Route 5 – Logroño to Mendavia (105km/65mi)

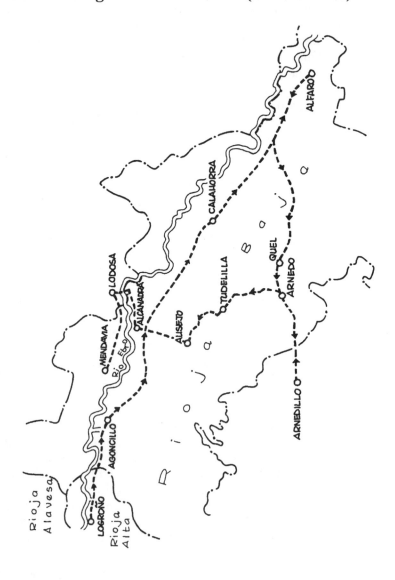

Route 5 takes you into the Rioja Baja, which is quite different from the Rioja Alta and the Rioja Alavesa. Its twisting roads run alongside steep gorges formed millions of years ago, through dramatic deserted mountains. The eagles soaring overhead are virtually your only companions, apart from the few cars you will meet that delight in roaring through the bends on the wrong side of the road (so take care!).

We leave Logroño on the N232 and head east for **Agoncillo**, where the River Leza runs into the River Ebro, with its 13th century *Castle of Aguas Mansas*, a national historical and artistic monument. The nearby *Church of Santa María* is an ornamented baroque building with a single nave, a graceful tower and integral side chapels, the central part of which was added in the 16th century. The beautiful Renaissance altarpiece shows scenes depicting the life of the Virgin and the Passion. The Roman road, which originally joined the eastern and western parts of Spain at León, runs parallel to the river all the way to Logroño, and is the site of many archaeological remains. Here ***Bodega Alejos*** (founded 1976) is built in the newer, contemporary style and welcomes visitors by appointment (English, French and German are spoken).

Continue along the N232 until you come to **Calahorra**, originally the Roman town of Calagurris, which is around 48km (30mi) from Logroño. This interesting town contains a typical 17th century Gothic church with a neo-classical façade and an 18th century tower, together with a museum containing a fascinating collection of sculptures and paintings. The baroque cathedral is a national monument with a triumphal archway and decorated elaborate rococo altarpieces to *San Pedro de la Epifanía* and *de la Visitación*. There is also the attractive 18th century baroque church of *Carmelitas Descalzas*.

The colourful market on Thursday is well worth a visit and also the newer style ***Bodega Coop San Isidro*** (founded in 1957). Hotels in Calahorra include the *Marco Fabio Quintiliano Parador*, one of Spain's premier chain of luxury hotels. Some 20km (13mi) downstream on the River Alhama, standing high on a hill overlooking cornfields and isolated vineyards, is **Alfaro**, once an important frontier town between Castile and the Kingdom of Navarre. It is of Roman origin and contains a number of ornate churches (including the 16th century *San Miguel*) and convents in the old town, with its vast colony of white storks (the largest in the world on a single building).

There are five bodegas in and around Alfaro, of which only **Bodegas Palacios Remondo** can be visited without an appointment. Founded in 1947, it has an 85-room hotel, swimming pool and four restaurants with a good culinary reputation. Daily visits are from 9am to 1pm and 4 to 7pm (closed in August), when you can visit the vineyards and cellars with 2,000 oak barrels, together with an interesting wine museum containing old vinification tools. English and French are spoken. **Bodegas Campo Burgo**, the oldest bodega in Alfaro, was founded in 1889 and includes some buildings dating from 1800 with one metre thick walls. The bodega is situated in the midst of 15ha (37 acres) of vineyards and gardens. English, French and Dutch are spoken.

Bodegas y Viñedos Ilurce, founded in 1940, is built in traditional Riojan style and has 200-year-old ageing cellars, in stark contrast to its modern vinification area (daily visits by appointment). **Bodegas Burgo Viejo** has an impressive fermentation chamber with a vaulted roof and can be visited by appointment on weekday mornings and afternoons (closed in August). English and French are spoken. **Torres-Librada** in **Estarijo** is surrounded by vineyards and housed in a building that was once an aircraft hanger on a military airfield. Weekday visits by appointment (French is spoken).

We now head back towards Logroño on the N232 and call in at **Aldeanueva de Ebro**, where the largest bodega in Rioja making its own wine is found, **Viñedos de Aldeanueva Coop**. They use outstanding oenological technology to make their wines from their 2,500ha (6,177 acres) of vineyards, which are aged in 6,000 oak barrels. They also have bullfights!

Continuing into the River Cidacos Valley on the LR115 we next stop at **Quel**, an impressive village situated beneath a vast rock face. Many dwellings are cut into the rock, with their roofs covered in vine shoots to cushion them against falling rocks. In the village, where basket weavers and wine-skin makers still ply their ancient trades, there is a 15th century castle (free entrance) overlooking the river valley and wine cellars cut into the rock on the more accessible river bank.

On 6th August the festival of 'bread and cheese' is held commemorating an event in 1479 when the plague decimated the population. The villagers asked the area's Saints for protection and 13 identical candles were lit each representing a Saint plus the Virgin de la Antigua and Our Lord Jesus Christ. The latter two candles lasted longest, with 'Christ's candle' being extinguished last of all. Ever since then, the villagers have organised a procession of thanksgiving to the Hermitage of Holy Christ of the Transfiguration on 6th August, while the Brotherhood makes a charitable offering of bread, cheese and wine, which are thrown from the hermitage's windows to the populace below.

Quel is famous for its snails (*caracoles*) and its huge variety of fruit, which can be purchased dried, as liqueurs or as delicious preserves. The Cidacos Valley offers an appetising variety of local dishes including snails cooked with *chorizo*, bacon and ham, with a touch of thyme and laurel, garnished with a hot dressing and served alongside a fried side dish. There are two bodegas in Quel, *Coop San Justo y Isidro* and *Bodegas Ontañón* (English spoken), which has a museum containing paintings and statues.

Continuing on the LR115 we come to **Arnedo**, just 2km from Quel on the left bank of the river Cidacos, where remains from the bronze age and Roman era have been found in the hills above the town. Arnedo is famous for the manufacture of footwear and its *Footwear Museum* is well worth a visit, as are a couple of interesting churches. It celebrates an annual festival of *The Robbery of the Saints* on 27th September, which links Arnedo with the Navarran villagers of San Adrián, Andosilla and other villages as they try to steal the Saints, carried on portable platforms, and take them back to Navarra. Finally, Arnedo win the day and keep their Saints. At *Bodega Faustino Rivero Ulecia* visitors are welcomed daily by appointment, with English and French spoken. The whole area abounds with legends, festivals, delicious food and Baja wines for your enjoyment.

Leaving Arnedo on the LR115 we arrive at **Arnedillo**, a famous spa town with a château-style bodega, *Santuario Vinícola Riojano*, built around a 300-year-old mill on the banks of the River Cidacos (less than 2km from the Arnedillo

Health Spa). Visitors are welcome between 10am and 8pm and no appointment is necessary (English and Japanese are spoken).

Returning to Arnedo on the LR115, just before reaching Quel turn left on to the LR123, followed shortly after by a another left onto the LR381 to **Tudelilla**, where you will find *Cosecheros de Tudelilla* (visits by appointment, mornings and afternoons). Continuing on the LR381 we come to the N232 where we turn left to **Ausejo**, an important wine town in the Rioja Baja (noted for its cultivated mushrooms) where *Coop Bodega San Miguel*, with its period architecture, is found. Ausejo is a typical fortified hill town dominated by a 13th century castle, where some rewarding time can be spent wandering through its interesting, winding streets.

Follow the LR348 to Alcanadre and turn left on to the NA134 to **Mendavia**, where *Bodegas Barón de Ley* is housed in a completely restored 16th century Benedictine monastery (a designated artistic monument) surrounded by vineyards. They produce modern-style wines using their own grapes and have weekday visits by appointment (English and French are spoken). To complete Wine Route 5, return to Logroño (18km/11mi) on the NA134.

The theme for *The Pilgrims' Way* (see page 143) in the year 2000 is 'Europe and the World'. Santiago de Compostela is welcoming pilgrims with a *Codex Calixtinus* mass on May 10th and various attractions are planned throughout the year in an attempt to attract more earthly (wealthy) tourists. The Compostela 2000 Office can be accessed via the Internet (⌨ www. compostela 2000.com, ✉ info@compostela2000).

Monastery & Bodega Route (60km/37mi)

The monastery and bodega route takes in many of Rioja's most beautiful and historic monasteries, with stops at a number of bodegas along the way. We start our journey at **Cenicero**, half way between Haro and Logroño on the N232, where we take the LR113 to **Uruñuela** and the baroque shrine of *La Virgen del Patrocinio*. Nearby is ***Bodega Leza García***, a small family bodega with traditional fermentation pools and a storage cave. Visits by appointment on Saturdays only, between 10.30am and 6pm (English and French are spoken).

Continue along the LR113 to **Nájera**, which was the main political centre of the re-conquest from the Moors between 923 and 1076 and the former seat of the kingdom of Pamplona-Nájera. King Sancho II *'El Grande'* built a new road to Santiago through Rioja and in 1052 his son added a hostel for pilgrims to the *Monasterío de Santa María La Real*, which had been founded 20 years earlier. Various kings and queens are buried in a great mausoleum in the walls of this well-preserved monastery, which is worth a visit. Opening times are from 9.30am to 1.30pm and 4 to 7.30pm daily (closed on Mondays during winter).

About 5km (3mi) south of Nájera, turn right on to the LR205 towards Cárdenas and then to **Badarán**, where there are two bodegas. *David Moreno Peña* welcomes visitors without an appointment from Mondays to Saturdays between 10am and 1.30pm and 4.30 to 7.30pm, and Sundays from 10am to 1.30pm (English, French and Italian are spoken), while visits to *Bodegas Larrea Merino* are weekdays by appointment. Badarán is just 6km (4mi) from the *Monastery of Cañas,* while the monasteries of *Suso* and *Yuso* (well signposted) are both situated 5km (3mi) from San Millán de la Cogolla and just 11km (7mi) from the ski resort of Valdezcaray.

This mountainous area is serenely peaceful and beautiful, and of important historical significance, as the oldest known documents written in Spanish and Basque were found in the libraries of the *Monastery of Yuso. Suso*, situated high in the wooded mountains, is a 10th century Mozarabic monastery, originally built to guard the cave where the Benedictine holy hermit, San Millán, lived in reclusion. He was reputed to have appeared on a white horse, like St. James the Apostle, to defend the Christians from the Moors, and is still worshipped widely in Rioja and Castile.

It is now decision time! From San Millán de la Cogolla you can either drive south for around 20km (12mi) higher into the Sierra de la Demanda mountains, to the *Monastery of Valvanera,* or north to the Cistercian *Monastery of Cañas* (*Santa María del Salvador*). For the latter, take the LR206 and after around 8km (5mi) you will arrive at the monastery, which was founded in 1169. It is a beautiful Gothic building with the altar windows designed to flood the interior with light, which

Saint Benedict found to have deep religious significance. Visits are both morning and afternoons and cost around 250 ptas.

Alternatively, you can drive to the *Monasterio de la Virgen de Valvanera*. Leave San Millán de la Cogolla on the road to Estollo and turn right at Bobadilla onto the LR113 and after 11km (7mi) turn right again onto the LR435 and Valvanera is just 4km (2.5mi) away. The monastery lies in an impressive setting in peaceful wooded mountains around 32km (20mi) from Cañas and 16km (10mi) from Anguiano, which is famous for its dancers on stilts.

The Pilgrims' Way to Santiago de Compostela

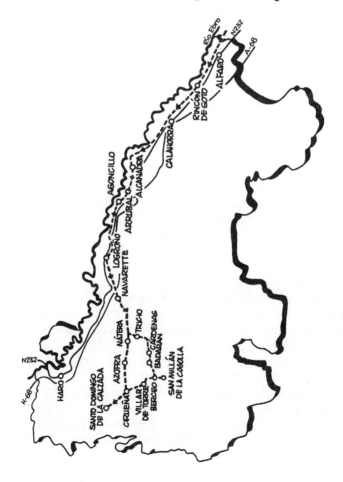

For hundreds of years *The Pilgrims' Way* from Le Puy (France) to Santiago de Compostela (Galicia) has been one of the main arteries of Europe's religious and cultural life, and, as it crosses Rioja, it is of tremendous historical and spiritual significance to the region. *The Way* was started in 950AD by Goldescalo, the Bishop of Le Puy (today credited as the first historically confirmed pilgrim) in the Auvergne (France). He travelled to Compostela where a new village was being built beside the tomb of the Apostle, St James, which had been discovered in 813AD. At the time Alfonso II El Casto reigned in Asturias and Charlemagne in Aix-la-Chappelle, and *The Way* has endured through the Romanesque, Gothic, Renaissance and Baroque periods to the present day. Pilgrims travel from far and wide to participate in this significant religious experience and hopefully earn themselves a place in heaven.

The pilgrims could be considered the first tourists and the world's first guidebook appeared in 1143AD, when Aimery Picaud produced the *Codex Calixtinus*. It described the complete itinerary including details of churches and hospices, good and bad waters, meals, and also the customs of the towns along the route. It even included a warning to 'refuse the offer of drinks from innkeepers and others, for they may be drugged as a prelude to robbery or even murder'! Today, all you face is the risk of seduction by Riojan food and wine – and sore feet!

Pilgrims entered Spain via several passes in the Pyrenees, crossing into the Rioja Baja at the town of **Alfaro**. Spiritually uplifted, pilgrims tramped wearily onwards from Alfaro to Rincón de Soto, Calahorra, Alcandre and Agoncillo, before arriving at **Logroño**. On level roads running through welcome orchards and green fields, they crossed over the River Ebro on the Puente de Piedra, a bridge designed by Juan de Ortega, the disciple of Santo Domingo. Meanwhile, Santiago de Compostela was still an awesome 666km (414mi) away! In medieval Logroño, they traversed the Rúa Vieja and Calle Mayor, where they stopped at the churches of *Santiago* and *Santa María del Palacio*.

Strengthened in body and soul by the hospitality of the local populace, they continued along *The Way* to **Navarette**, where there was a pilgrims' hospice run by the Order of St. John. On the same paved way used by early pilgrims, a statue of St.

James on horseback can still be seen today in the niche of an old mansion, together with the ruins of a Romanesque shrine. At the sides of the road to **Alesón** are the tumbling ruins of the *Convent of San Antón* and *The Templar*. Next stop was **Nájera**, the historical capital of Rioja, which reached its greatest splendour under the Kings of Navarre. Directed by Sancho the Great, who was responsible for *The Way* passing through Nájera instead of its previous route through the Basque Country, coins were minted at Nájera for the very first time. The 11th century *Convent of Santa María la Real* contains superb cloisters, choir stalls and the tombs of several Kings of Navarre, Castile and León.

Here the pilgrims turned off *The Way* towards **San Millán de La Cogolla** in the south to visit the famous monasteries of *Yuso* and *Suso* (see pages 115 and 141). The pilgrims rejoined *The Way* at **Berceo**, the birthplace of the poet Gonzalo de Berceo (who sang the miracles of Our Lady), famous as the first poet known to use the Castilian language.

Santo Domingo de la Calzada, founded in the second half of the 11th century, is the last stage of *The Way* in the Rioja region. Here a hermit and holy man made his home in a wood on the bank of the River Oja near to the where the pilgrims used to cross. Having seen their difficulties, he set about repairing the roads, building a bridge and installing a hospice in his former hermitage, and the town became known as Santo Domingo de la Calzada. In the 14th century, *Pedro the Cruel*, King of Castile, built walls around the town to provide protection. Among the many fine old buildings are *Santo Domingo's Cathedral*, a blend of styles although largely Gothic with a baroque spire, the *Hermitage of Nuestra Senora de la Plaza*, a Romanesque-style church and the *Convent of San Francisco*, with the beautiful but somewhat austere lines of the Herrera style.

The *Pilgrims' Way* has been an inspiration for centuries and still attracts thousands of pilgrims – on foot, horseback or, nowadays, even bicycle – all eager to visit the tomb of St. James. They return home spiritually uplifted with happy memories of friendly people, a land of castles, fortified churches and noble manors (not forgetting celebrated vineyards) in a beautiful setting.

¡Que Aproveche!

5.

ENJOYING WINE

> 'Wine rejoices the heart of man, and joy is the mother of all virtues.'
>
> Goethe.

Goethe was spot on! Wine is one of life's great pleasures, whether drinking it, tasting it, enjoying it with friends, talking about it and even learning about it. You will become familiar with geography, geology, grapes, soils, climate, history and also make friends with many like-minded enthusiasts. You may even live longer with all this enjoyment and relaxation!

Buying Wine

The enjoyment of wine starts with its purchase, which should be a pleasure – whether searching for bargains, buying old favourites or trying new wines. You can buy wine from numerous specialist wine shops, supermarkets, wine clubs, mail order and even over the Internet – the possibilities are endless. Before buying wine from a retail outlet, check how it is stored and displayed, particularly the older, better quality wines. Bottles displayed standing up, at high temperatures or in sunlight will obviously not be in peak condition and should be avoided. Take care in the hot summer months when travelling to Rioja or the continent in your car to buy wine, as it will be subjected to excessive heat and will probably be ruined. It is far better to visit in the cooler months, when the locals will also be more welcoming as it will be less busy.

Storing Wine

If you plan to store wine for any length of time, it is advisable to have some wine racks in a suitable storage area with the bottles lying down. This allows the cork to remain in contact with the wine and prevents it from drying out. The natural porosity of the cork allows a tiny amount of air into the wine, enabling it to slowly age and mature, which is why Riojan wines aged in oak before bottling continue to age (and improve) further in the bottle. Man-made stoppers (e.g. plastic) do not allow this small but significant ingress of air into the bottle necessary to mature quality wines.

Not many of us live in homes that are ideal for wine storage, but you should at least ensure that the area chosen is vibration free or your wine will age faster. The temperature should never fall below 5°C (41°F) or rise above 20°C (68°F) and should ideally be kept at a constant 7-10°C (45-50°F) with ventilation and reasonable humidity to avoid mustiness. Keeping wine in the kitchen or near a sunny window or any heat source will ruin it in double-quick time. If you do not have a cellar or cool storage place in your home, you can buy a temperature-controlled wine storage cabinet, with a capacity of from around 50 to over 250 bottles (although they are relatively expensive).

Note that the period of time a wine can be stored before it starts to deteriorate varies considerably depending on the type and style of wine, how it was made, the grapes used, how long it has been aged, the year and the producer. In general, young un-aged wines needs to be drunk within a year or two of production, *crianzas* are good for up to 7 years, *reservas* up to 12 years and *gran reservas* up to 20 years. These are actual figures provided by **Lan, Bodegas** as indicated on their bottles, although they are necessarily a only a *rough* guide.

Any wine (even cheaper varieties) transported for long periods in a vehicle and consequently severely shaken, should be left for a few weeks to settle down. There is some disagreement on this point, but if your are in any doubt, the next time you buy wine abroad, drink a bottle immediately on arriving home and then sample another bottle in a month's time – and note the difference!

Serving Wine

When you open a bottle of wine it is exposed to air and is 'breathing' or being aerated or oxidised. This slow oxidation happens naturally in the corked bottle (in the process called maturation) when the various compounds present mature with time. Opening the bottle speeds up this process, which explains why you should not let very old wine breathe for too long. It will go 'go over the hill' and could be a very expensive lesson!

All red wines should be allowed to breathe before drinking, with young full-bodied reds benefiting most. When serving more than one wine, it is important that you serve the younger and/or lesser quality wines before the better ones, otherwise they will taste even more inferior.

The enjoyment of wine drinking is greatly enhanced by serving it at the correct temperature – in fact the temperature at which a wine is served is *crucial* and the single most important influence on how it will taste. Red *gran reservas* and *reservas* should be served at just below room temperature (18-19°C/64-66°F) and *crianzas* at a slightly lower temperature (16°C/61°F) in good-sized wine glasses, not overly full. The wine can then be properly swirled to release its bouquet and increase your enjoyment. Whites and rosés should generally be served cooler, but not too cold – around 8-11°C (46-52°F) for whites and 6-8°C (43-46°F) for rosés – and sweeter wines a little cooler. The exception is traditional oak-aged whites, which are better served at the higher temperature of 12-14°C (54-57°F).

It is advisable to take wine out of the cooler wine storage area well before serving, in order to allow it to warm up naturally. Artificial heating (e.g. in warm water or in front of a fire) is not advisable, although warm glasses help, as you can lose a degree or two simply by pouring wine into a cold glass. If wine (red or white) is served too cold, a widespread practice, you can place your hands around the bowl to warm it up. The colder the wine, the less bouquet is released and the more you will register tannin and acidity; conversely the warmer the wine, the less you will register tannin and acidity and the more the bouquet will be released.

Wines with lots of fruity bouquet, such as red Riojan *jóvenes,* can, however, usefully be served cool – splendidly refreshing on a hot day – while sparkling wines such as Spanish Cavas served cold retain their bubbles longer. As a rough guide, light sweet whites and sparkling whites can be chilled in a refrigerator for two hours, light and sparkling reds, light dry whites, medium bodied whites and full sweet whites for one and a half hours, while fuller dry whites need only around one hour. The preferable way, however, is to cool your wines in a wine bucket half-filled with ice, or use rapid-chill sheaths which are stored in a freezer and then slipped over the bottle before serving.

Although it is not common practice in Rioja, you can pour wine into a jug or decanter to aerate and age it, which will certainly improve the taste of cheap red wines. As a last resort, you can mix it with sparkling mineral water, soda water or even lemonade to make the refreshing *tinto de verano* (literally 'summer red') wine drink. However, do not cook with cheap wine as it will ruin the taste of food. It goes without saying that the above applies only to *cheap* red wine!

Tasting Wine

Although tasting wine falls into various categories, the basic techniques remain the same. Wine in a restaurant is tasted to check for faults, not for studying, and if there is something wrong it will be replaced. Similarly, faulty wine bought from a shop should be returned for replacement or a refund. If you are tasting wine to buy or are at home with friends, remember the wine trade adage 'buy on an apple, sell on cheese'. Dry biscuits or bread are the best accompaniment, remembering to spit out rather than swallow if you are driving or are offered a lot of wines to try, otherwise your palate soon becomes tired and undiscerning.

It is important to have an open mind when tasting wines for the first time, because in addition to checking for faults you are trying to determine whether you like it. It follows that you should try not to be influenced by other people, fancy labels or even reputations, vividly illustrated by a true story from Rioja involving the respected and prestigious **Marqués de Riscal**.

In the first edition (1988) of the superb **Sotheby's Wine Encyclopaedia**, *Marqués de Riscal* wines were described as having an unpleasant, musty mushroom character. This information was conveyed back to Francisco Hurtado de Amexaga at Riscal, who immediately recalled his top winemaker from Rueda to investigate. To his credit, even though Hurtado de Amexaga was unsure whether or not this was true, he conceded that if the mustiness had crept in over a long period the wines could have developed a 'cellar palate' that they had failed to notice.

In fact, the wines had gradually acquired this musty character since the '60s. However, being one of the oldest Riojan bodegas with the reputation of being in the top three, no one had dared to mention it (a reminder of the story of 'the emperor's clothes'). The wine in every one of their barrels (20,000!) was tasted and 2,000 were immediately destroyed – the equivalent of 600,000 bottles poured down the drain! A further 2,000 borderline barrels were earmarked for replacement the following year and a programme initiated to renew all 20,000 barrels over the next decade. As a result, the 1988 vintage had a pureness of fruit not seen in any Riscal wines since the '60s and the following 1989 and 1990 vintages, with their combination of superior wine and the (now increased) new oak content, made a discernible difference to the taste. *Marqués de Riscal's* position among the world's great wines was justifiably regained with this no-expense-spared dedication to quality.

The moral of the story is therefore not to be a slave to reputations when tasting and to have the courage of knowing what you like. Tasting (and drinking) wines should be one of life's pleasures and can be compared to appreciating anything

artistic. You may appreciate certain music, dance or art, for example, but may not be able to describe exactly why in technical terms, and the same applies to wine tasting. The message is not only to savour the wine, but also to savour the delightful thought that with greater experience, drinking wine will become ever more pleasurable.

Firstly, to assess wine you need to use a glass of the right size, a clear glass – no etched dancing nymphs please – and a bowl with the rim going inwards in a tulip shape, enabling the wine to be swirled and the released bouquet to be retained in the glass. Wine buffs and aspiring wine buffs may wish to buy the thin, plain, crystal glasses designed by the Austrian Georg Riedel, who fervently believes that how the wine hits the tongue affects its taste. He has designed wine glasses for dozens of different wine types – even for young as opposed to older wine! However, they are *very* expensive and contradict the idea of unpretentious wine enjoyment.

Fill the glass less than half full and hold it at the base of the stem (not with your hands around the bowl) – just examining the wine will impart valuable information, which is why the glass needs to be clear. Tilt the glass away from you against a white background and examine the edge of the wine, where the variations in colour will reveal its age. Red wines vary between a brown, brick-red colour for older wines to deep purple for young ones, with varying shades in between. White wines, on the other hand, vary between a pale, yellowy-green colour in young wines to deep gold in older wines, caused by oxidation in the ageing process. Good quality wines also have an attractive radiance.

The stem of the glass enables it to be held without covering the bowl and also allows the wine to be swirled effectively to release its bouquet. When the swirling stops, look at the fine film of wine slowly descending the glass, called 'the legs', the movement and appearance signifying the quality and, with practice, the wine's alcoholic strength. It is important to fill the glass less than half full for two very good reasons: the first is to stop the wine being propelled *out* of the glass (!) and the second is to retain the released bouquet *in* the glass.

Sniff the bouquet and try to concentrate on it, because a lot of taste is actually contained in the smell – check that the wine has no unpleasant smells and also decide what it reminds you of, mentally storing this information away for the future (some people use a notebook). Grapes, and therefore wine, contain a myriad of compounds, with the flavours being enhanced by the vinification and maturation process in oak barrels. Describing wines is a challenge requiring complex observations to be committed to memory, which can be daunting – but remember you are doing it for pleasure!

Take a mouthful and really swirl it around your mouth in order to make contact with your taste buds. The acidity will register on the upper edges of the tongue, the sweetness on the tip of the tongue, and if there is a bitter taste, on the flat back part of the tongue. The tannin content from the grape skins, pips and sometimes the stems, affects the inside of your cheeks and, if excessive, will have an unpleasant astringency similar to drinking stewed tea! Drawing in air at the same time not only sounds delightfully rude, but ensures that some of the bouquet is drawn into the nasal passages to be analysed by your brain. At the same time, note how the fullness or body of the wine actually feels in your mouth and then either spit it out or swallow it.

At this final stage, as the brain's analytical processes come into play, it is fascinating to watch the facial expressions of an expert taster. They appear to be in a daydream as they appraise every facet of the wine, including its balance and how long its effect lasts in the mouth after being swallowed. This effect is called the finish – fleeting in a lesser quality wine or as long as 30 seconds in quality wine. The whole tasting process enables you to give your verdict on the wine and is even more enjoyable when tasting good quality wines and sharing the experience with wine-loving friends.

Wine Faults

Winemaking is a complex art and it is hardly surprising that sometimes there are problems – assessment of wine quality is subjective making objectivity difficult! What in general terms are faults, can be a virtue in certain cases. Champagne and Cava production are prime examples, as the secondary fermentation that produces the 'fizz' is certainly not acceptable in other wines, while the wonderful luscious sweetness of Sauternes depends on the mould growth of the *botrytis cinerea* fungus, which elsewhere can be disastrous.

In the main, although faulty wines are unpleasant they will not harm you, unless of course (as has happened in the past in some countries) they have been deliberately contaminated to increase profit. The inherent alcohol and acidity stop the growth of bacteria, although some compounds that may be present will detract from the enjoyment of wine. This section is designed to help you recognise and understand these features.

Corked, corkiness or cork taint is an unpleasant musty or mouldy smell and is not to be confused with bits of cork floating around in your wine glass from a badly opened bottle or when a cork disintegrates. The problem arises due to cork mould and, for the technically minded, the presence of 2, 4, 6 trichloroanisole seems to be the culprit, as it is leached out of the cork and occasionally oak barrels, into the wine. It is a powerful-smelling chemical and only 5ml (a teaspoonful) would contaminate the entire Spanish annual wine production!

As wine drinking increases and people become more knowledgeable, the incidence of corked wine seems to be increasing and it is estimated that as many as one in ten bottles may be affected. As a consequence, a move away from bark corks has begun, and inert, man-made corks and metal screw-tops have been developed. However, these provoke a furore in traditional wine-producing regions – simply mentioning them to some Riojan wine-makers turns them wine coloured!

Hydrogen sulphide is the rotten egg smell from school chemistry laboratories, which, although unsafe in very high concentrations, is not a health hazard in wines. It is caused by the fermentation of some strains of yeast and requires nitrogen and specific conditions for it to accumulate.

Oxidation is caused by oxygen reacting with other components in the winemaking process, and can result in the same problem as wine drinking – a little is beneficial and too much can be a disaster. Uncontrolled oxidation can take place during storage, in the bottling process and also in bottles with faulty corks or stoppers. Unintentional oxidation in white wine changes its colour and taste, with the wine said to be 'maderised'. *Do not drink it.*

"There's no wine in heaven, let's drink it here on earth."

Proverb

In *Madeira* wine production, intentional oxidation is induced and its production is one of a number of fascinating stories over the centuries of 'accidents' producing unexpected results. The brandy added to Madeira to stop fermentation and to keep it sweet on its two crossings of the equator (it was carried as ballast in sailing ships) hastened its long maturing process and fortuitously produced wonderful wine. These long sea voyages have now been replaced by the *estufa* system, which replicates the tropical heat of ship-borne travels by warming the wine for four or five months to 120°F (49°C) in *estufas* (hot stores), giving Madeira its characteristic caramel tang.

Sulphur dioxide has been used in winemaking since Roman times and is unmatched as a preservative, but problems arise when it is used to excess. A sharp prickly sensation in the nose then becomes apparent and some asthmatics react badly to it, so much so, that in certain countries (including the USA) a warning is included on labels. The use of sulphur dioxide is more prevalent in white than red wines, and rigorous quality control during production is necessary to avoid problems.

Volatile acidity describes the presence of excessive acetic acid, otherwise known as vinegar, and the related ethyl acetate found in nail varnish – neither of which are recommended ingredients of wine! It is produced under certain conditions during fermentation and therefore normally controlled in good winemaking practices. It is not to be confused with the natural acidity produced by malic and tartaric acids in grape juice, which impart the refreshing flavour and balance to many wines. In Rioja, the white grape Viura, which is acidic, is sometimes added to red wines to balance the wine and provide the necessary acidity.

Most faults can be spotted immediately wine is poured and you only need to observe it in a (clear) wine glass, swirl it and smell it, for the faults to become glaringly obvious. Happily, just a small percentage of wines are affected.

Washing Wine Glasses: If you use washing up liquid, always use it sparingly and rinse the glasses well with clear water, as the residue will alter the taste of the wine, and in the case of sparkling wines, will destroy the effervescent bubbles. Be warned!

Wine & Health

Drink wine for pleasure, gratefully accepting that the enjoyment and the flavanoids will probably prolong your life. These flavanoids, or anti-oxidants 'mop-up' the harmful chemicals in the body and reputedly fight heart disease, cancer and brain degenerating diseases such as Alzheimer's and Parkinson's, and are present in all red wine. They are found naturally on the skins of grapes and current research suggests that they are present in greater volume in small, thick-skinned varieties grown in hot climates.

Tempranillo, the main grape used in Riojan reds, and Graciano (which is also commonly used) are both thick-skinned red grapes, and therefore should help you live a longer, healthier life. The obvious proviso is that you drink wine in moderation with food and not on an empty stomach. As well as single-grape (varietal) Tempranillo wines, there are now varietal Graciano reds from *Bodegas SMS* and *Viña Ijalba*, with the grapes from the latter grown in their own vineyards using organic methods, providing a double health benefit! Cabernet Sauvignon, although not an official Riojan grape variety, is also high in flavanoids. You should also bear in mind the following:

• Regular moderate drinking is healthier than occasional heavy bouts or even abstinence.

- The optimum intake is two average size drinks a day or less for a woman (most women can drink only two-thirds as much as men).

- Drinking with meals reduces the risk of liver disease.

- Drinking before a meal stimulates the appetite and numbs the signals to the brain telling you that you are full, so you will eat more.

- Drinking excess alcohol increases the risk of mouth and throat cancers.

- Wine contains flavanoids that can protect against cancer, but not if you drink more than a couple of glasses daily.

- Bubbly drinks help alcohol enter the bloodstream more quickly.

- The liver takes one hour to metabolise and get rid of one unit of alcohol.

> **"Drinking a glass of wine with your meal is a peseta less for the physician."**
>
> **Spanish Proverb**

Wine & Food

Matching food and wine is one of life's pleasures and trying different combinations to suit your palate should be an enjoyable experience. The following tips are designed to help you with this process, although you should never forget that what *you* like is all that counts (the same applies when tasting wines). Acidic citrus fruits and any type of vinegar, even tomatoes, will ruin the taste of wines and this includes mint sauce made with vinegar and served with lamb – in fact all sweet chutneys are best avoided with older wines. Freshly ground pepper with mature reds will do them no favours, while sweet wines should be sweeter than the food they are being served with, and hot curries will devastate the taste of any wine, although milder curries or savouries are perfectly acceptable with a sweetish white. Even red wine with fish is 'acceptable' – but not with smoked salmon and asparagus, as both are prone to taste metallic with red wine.

> **"I like best the wine drunk at the expense of others."**
>
> **Diogenes 'The Cynic'**

Riojan *crianza, reserva* and *gran reserva* red wines are an ideal complement to meat dishes, chicken and even the spicy *chorizo* sausage found in La Rioja. The classic *platos riojanos* – *patatas riojanos, pimientos asados* or *chuletas al sarmiento* (small milk-fed lamb chops cooked over vine shoots) and cheeses all go well with aged reds. The local young (*joven*) fruity, juicy reds fit the bill for the various local *tapas*, but are not so good with cheeses. Strong cheeses will devastate fine wine and acidic or sweet white wines are often better.

A few suggestions for cooking with wine:

- Never cook with wine that is 'off' – if you cannot drink it, do not cook with it. Also you should not cook with cheap inferior wine as it will ruin the taste of food.

- Avoid aluminium saucepans as they cause food to darken when wine is used.

- You should under-salt recipes cooked with wine as the natural salts and minerals concentrate with the cooking, making food excessively salty – always taste food and then add more seasoning at the end if required.

- Never add cold wine to hot food as it will lower the cooking temperature.

- Simmer wine before adding to food to reduce the volume of liquid and also considerably reduce it when using eggs, butter or cream. Heat gently and do not let the sauce boil. (Note that double cream is the only cream that will stand boiling.)

- Wine loses its alcohol when cooked, leaving the flavour in the finished dish.

- Wine is also the basis of good stock and is a good marinade with which to tenderise food.

La Catedral de Calahorra

APPENDICES

APPENDIX A: ACCOMMODATION

In these appendices (and elsewhere in this book) the following symbols have been used: ✆ (telephone), 🖷 (fax), 🖳 (Internet) and ✉ (e-mail).

Hotels

There are over 120 hotels in La Rioja. All three of Rioja's wine sub-regions are within a compact area and therefore it is possible to be based in one hotel (or camp site) and make daily excursions, which saves uprooting yourself and packing and unpacking suitcases. The following are a few suggestions, with prices ranging from 6,000 to 14,000 ptas per night for a double room. A more comprehensive selection is available from local tourist offices (see page 204).

Alfaro (Rioja Baja): Bodegas Palacios (Ctra. Zaragossa, ✆ 941 180 100, 🖷 941 247 798) has its own 2-star hotel (Palacios Rioja) with 85-bedrooms, a good restaurant and a swimming pool. There is also a wine museum containing old vinification tools.

Arnedo (Rioja Baja): Hotel Virrey (27 Paseo de la Constitución, ✆ 941 380 150) is a comfortable hotel with a moderately priced restaurant serving local cuisine and wines.

Briñas (Rioja Alta): The 3-star Hospedería Señorío de Briñas (✆ 941 304 224, 🖷 941 304 345 ✉ hsbrinas@ arrakis.es) has modern en-suite facilities and olde-worlde charm with friendly owners, and is a convenient base to explore the area and its bodegas. Breakfast is included in the room rate. There are also two restaurants in this interesting wine village situated on the N124 to Vitoria (3km from Haro).

Calahorra (Rioja Baja): The Marco Fabio Quintiliano (✆ 941 130 358, 🖷 941 135 139) is a 3-star *parador*, part of the government-owned luxury hotel chain. Its restaurants specialise in local dishes with a good selection of Riojan wines.

Most Paradors offer a 35 per cent discount (at various times of the year) to those aged over 60. For details of offers, ☎ 915 166 666, 🖷 915 166 657, ✉ info@parador.es, 🖳 www.parador.es

Haro (Rioja Alta): Hotel Los Agustinos (2 Plaza San Augustín (☎ 941 311 308, 🖷 941 312 413) is a well-known 4-star hotel conveniently situated for the numerous restaurants and *tapas* bars in the area known as *La Herradura* (the horseshoe). Hotel Iturrimurri (Ctra. 232, ☎ 941 311 213, 🖷 941 311 721) is a 4-star hotel situated on the main road from Haro to Logroño.

Laguardia (Rioja Alavesa): Hotel Restaurante Marixa (☎ 941 600 165 🖷 941 600 202) is a small, friendly hotel with ten air-conditioned, en suite bedrooms, some with panoramic views over the surrounding vineyards and mountains. Its excellent restaurant has an extensive range of Riojan wines and is open to non-residents. Hotel Castillo el Collado (☎ 941 121 200, 🖷 941 600 878) is a small, intimate hotel with eight elegant and tranquil bedrooms. The owner, Javier Arcillona, has restored this old mansion in an interesting and distinctive style and prepares the excellent food himself, needless to say, accompanied by an interesting selection of Riojan wines. For a romantic stay, why not book the 'love and madness' (*Amor y Locura*) room – but book early!

Logroño (Rioja Alta): The capital of La Rioja has a large selection of hotels including the Hotel Murrieta (1 Marqués de Murrieta, ☎ 941 224 150, 🖷 941 223 213, ✉ hotels@pretur. es). This is a 3-star hotel with 113 en-suite bedrooms, conveniently situated for the old Calle Laurel area of *tapas* bars and restaurants. Hotel Ciudad de Logroño (9 Menéndez Pelayo, ☎ 941 250 244, 🖷 941 254 390, ✉ hotels@pretur.es) is a 3-star hotel in the centre with 95 en-suite bedrooms, some overlooking a park. The Hotel Carlton Rioja (5 Gran Via, ☎ 941 242 100, 🖷 041 243 502, ✉ hotels@pretur.es) is 4-star with 88 double and 20 single rooms, plus various suites. The above three hotels all provide underground parking for around 1,500 ptas per day.

San Millán de la Cogolla (Rioja Alta) has two monasteries, *Suso* monastery, high in the mountains, and *Yuso* monastery, one wing of which has been converted into the Hostería del Monasterio de San Millán (☎ 941 373 277, 🖷 941 373 266, ✉ hosteria@sanmillan.com, 🖳 www.sanmillan.com). It is a 4-star, 25-bedroom luxury hotel, set amid stunning natural beauty on the *Pilgrims' Way*. The hotel's San Augustín Restaurant offers a tempting variety of local dishes and wines.

Santa Domingo de la Calzada, situated just outside the Rioja Alta sub-region, is home to the 4-star *Parador de Santo Domingo de la Calzada* (① 941 340 300, 📠 941 340 325), situated just outside the Rioja Alta area, which was originally a 12th century hospice for travellers on the *Pilgrims' Way*.

APPENDIX B: RESTAURANTS

The well-known Spanish proverb, 'three Spaniards, four opinions', does not apply to Riojanos and food – they unanimously agree that good wholesome cooking using local produce cooked in the traditional way is the only way to dine. Rioja's gastronomy is influenced by the wealth of fruit and vegetables grown in local market gardens, which together with the region's excellent meat and game and an abundance of fresh fish (both from the Atlantic and local rivers), means that every meal is a memorable occasion.

Delicious lamb chops, roast leg of lamb, young goat (*cabrito*), which skip straight off the hills into the ovens, rabbit, partridge, quail and a variety of small game in season, add to the wonderful variety of mouth-watering dishes. The ever popular piquant paprika sausages (*chorizos*) are enjoyed both as a starter and a main course, and also in the celebrated *patatas a la Riojanas*, a delicious 'hot-pot' of potatoes, *chorizo*, garlic, onion and peppers, the latter sometimes served on a separate plate. The vegetable dish, *menestra de verdura*, is made from local vegetables in season, asparagus, peas and artichokes, complemented with cured ham, *chorizo* and eggs. *Pochas Riojanas* not only contains *chorizo* but also haricot beans, and, if you like strong peppers, try *pimentos rellenos a la Riojanas* or the full-flavoured dish, *callos a la Riojana* made with *chorizo*, tripe, ham and nuts. *Pimientos asados* is a dish of red peppers fried with olive oil and garlic. *Lechazo asado* or *cordero lechal asado* is another classic, consisting of young milk-fed lamb, rubbed with garlic and roasted in a hot wood-fired oven until tender – absolutely delicious!

Surprisingly, in this venerable wine region, *solomillo al vino de Rioja*, beefsteak macerated in red Rioja and brandy, and cooked with small tasty onions and mushrooms, is one of the few regional dishes actually cooked with wine. *Chuletas* or the smaller *chuletillos al sarmiento* from very young lamb are delicious chops grilled over vine shoot embers. Fish is not neglected: trout and freshwater crayfish from local rivers, and Atlantic hake (*merluza*), cooked in a variety of ways, and *Bacalao a la Riojana*, and salted cod with red peppers and tomatoes, are just a few of the local offerings. With all these (and many more) mouth-watering dishes and the abundance of superb Riojan wine, it is little wonder that Riojans are such enthusiastic diners, whether at home or when dining out.

The following are just a small selection from the hundreds of restaurants in the region, some of which have been in existence for well over 100 years. There are over 100 restaurants in Logroño alone, almost all are informal and offering excellent value for money. Prices start as low as 1,000 ptas per person for the menu of the day (*menú de dia*) and often include wine, while moderately-priced menus cost around 2,000 ptas and 5,000 ptas would provide a veritable feast. Note that the majority do not open until 9pm or sometimes even later.

TIPPING: all prices and bills include service. If you wish to tip to express appreciation of good service it is customary to add no more than 5 per cent, although this is obviously a matter of personal preference.

Alfaro:

- Asador San Roque, San Roque (local Riojan specialities). An *asador* specialises in serving wood-roasted meat.

Arnedo:

- Casa Sopitas, 4 Carretera, (moderately priced, atmospheric restaurant serving authentic classical Riojan dishes and wines of the Rioja Baja).

Briñas:

- Bodegón Ayala (local specialities).
- Mesón Chomín (simple inexpensive local dishes).

Briones:

- Los Merendero (inexpensive classic Riojan food).

Calahorra:

- Casa Mateo, 15 Plaza del Raso (good value, excellent *chuletas* and good wines).
- Chef Niño, 1 C/Basconia (authentic food at reasonable prices).
- La Taberna de la Cuarta Esquina, 16 Cuatro Esquinas (another good value restaurant with innovative cooking).

Ezcaray:

- Echaurren, 2 Héroes del Alcázar (modern and traditional dishes from a 100-year-old, family-run restaurant).
- El Rincón del Vino, 2 Jesús Nazareno (3-star restaurant serving local specialities).

Fuenmayor:

- El Valenciano, 20 Avda. Cenicero (Valencian rice dishes and the Riojan speciality of roast kid cooked in a wood-fired brick oven).
- Donal, Pza. Azpilicueta (inexpensive local food and wines).
- Mesón Chuchi, 2 Carretera Vitoria (roasted and grilled meat and fish and an excellent wine list). They also have a wine shop.

Haro:

- Beethoven 1, 10 Santo Tomás (an Haro institution, informal with excellent *tapas*).
- Beethoven 11, 3-5 Santo Tomás (smarter than Beethoven 1 above, with the same excellent food and an extensive wine list).
- La Kika, 11 Santo Tomás (favoured by wine producers, so book early – traditional, well cooked, inexpensive food).
- Mesón Atamuri, 1 Pl. Juan Gato, just off the main square (excellent food with wines mainly from Haro's bodegas).
- Casa Terete, 26 General Franco (established in 1867 and little changed – inexpensive, authentic Riojan cooking served on scrubbed tables, accompanied by wines mostly from Haro's bodegas).

Logroño:

- La Merced (elegant, traditional restaurant with excellent food and an impressive selection of Riojan wines).

- La Chatilla de San Agustín, 2 Peso (above average prices, but an excellent restaurant serving Riojan specialities with a good wine list).

- Asador La Chata, 6 Carnicerías (established 1821).

- Cachetero, 3 Calle Laurel (traditional Riojan specialities but prepared to innovate – justly famous for over 100 years).

- El Charro, Calle Laurel (simple bar/restaurant with excellent inexpensive *chuletas, ensalada* and *pimientos*).

- Casa Matute, 6 Calle Laurel (inexpensive basic home-made food).

- Hotel Carlton Rioja, 5, Gran Via (well-known hotel restaurant, moderately priced local food with good Riojan wine list).

- El Rincón del Vino, 136 Marqués de San Nicolás (atmospheric and friendly cave restaurant with good, moderately priced Riojan food and wine).

- Bodegón El Refugio, 1 Labradores, La Zona (very popular and inexpensive specialising in *jamón y lomo ibérico*, cheeses and sausages, with a wide selection of Riojan wines).

- La Unión, 15 San Agustín (small and friendly serving home-cooked local specialities).

Laguardia:

- Hotel Marixa (moderately priced good traditional Basque and Riojan dishes, good selection of Riojan wines).

Labastida:

- El Bodegón (inexpensive, simple tasty food with their own *viño de cosechero*).

Nájera:

- El Mono, 6 Mayor (good value Riojan specialities).

Ollauri:

- Mesón Merche, 2 Mayor (inexpensive home cooking).

Oyón:

- Mesón la Cueva (popular, classic moderately-priced Riojan food, including wood-fired *lechazo asado*).

San Domingo de la Calzada:

- Mesón el Peregrino, 18 Zumalacárregui (moderately priced authentic food).

> A large number of bodegas have private dining rooms, which are primarily used for convivial get togethers of wine-loving friends and for entertaining groups.

APPENDIX C: MENU GUIDE

Vegetales (vegetables)

Alcachofas	Artichoke
Apio	Celery
Berenjenas	Aubergine
Berros	Watercress
Brócoli	Broccoli
Calabacines	Courgettes
Calabaza	Pumpkin, marrow
Cebolla	Onion
Cebolletas	Spring onions
Coles de Bruselas	Brussel sprouts
Coliflor	Cauliflower
Champiñónes	Mushrooms
Endibias	Endives
Ensalada	Salad
" (Mixta/Verde)	mixed/green salad
" (Rusa)	Russian Salad
Espárragos	Asparagus
Espinacas	Spinach
Guisantes	Peas
Judías verdes	French beans
Lechuga	Lettuce
Lombarda	Red cabbage
Menestra de verdura	Mixed vegetables
Nabos	Turnip
Patatas	Potatoes
Patatas fritas	Chips
Pepino	Cucumber
Pimientos	Sweet peppers
Pimientos a la Riojana	Red peppers stuffed with mince
Pisto	Ratatouille
Puerros	Leeks
Rábanos	Radish

Remolacha	Beetroot
Repollo	Cabbage
Tomate	Tomato
Zanahoria	Carrot

Legumbres (pulses)

Alubias	Kidney beans
Garbanzos	Chickpeas
Habas	Broad beans
Judías blancos	Haricot beans
Lentejas	Lentils

Sopas (soups)

Sopa de ajo	Garlic soup
Sopa de arroz	Rice soup
Sopa de cangrejos	Crayfish soup
Sopa de cebolla	Onion soup
Sopa gallego	Cabbage and haricot beans soup
Sopa Juliana	Clear soup of finely cut vegetables
Sopa de mariscos	Shellfish soup
Sopa de picadillo	Chicken, chopped sausage, egg noodles soup
Sopa de rabo de buey	Oxtail soup
Sopa de verdura	Vegetable soup
Sopa de fideos	Vermicelli soup
Sopa de pescado	Fish soup
Sopa de tortuga	Turtle soup
Puré	Thick soup
Consomé	Consommé
Consomé al Jerez	With sherry.
Gazpacho	Can vary, but is generally tomato, green peppers, onion, bread, garlic, oil and vinegar, and is always served cold.

Carne (meat)

Albóndigas	Meat balls
Anojo	Yearling
Bistec	Steak
Buey	Beef
Cabrito	Kid
Callos	Tripe
Carne adobada	Marinated meat
Carne asada	Roast meat
Carne blanca	White meat
Carne roja	Red meat
Carnero	Mutton
Costillas	Ribs
Cerdo	Pork
Chuletas	Chops
Cochinillo	Suckling pig
Cordero	Lamb
Entrecot	Entrecote
Escalopines	Escalope
Estofado	Stew/Casserole
Fiambre	Cold meat
Filete	Fillet steak
Hígado	Liver
Jamón york	Boiled ham
Jamón serrano	Cured ham
Lengua	Tongue
Mollejas	Sweetbread, gizzards
Manos de cerdo	Pigs trotters
Manos de ternera	Calves feet
Morcilla	Black pudding
Riñones	Kidney
Salchichas	Sausages
Sesos	Brains
Solomillo	Sirloin
Solomillo de cerdo	Tenderloin

Ternera	Veal, but *chuleta de ternera* can be any grilled meat
Solomillo	Can describe tenderloin or fillet.

Caza (game)

Conejo	Rabbit
Cordonices	Quail
Corzo	Roe deer
Faisán	Pheasant
Jabalí	Wild boar
Liebre	Hare
Perdiz	Partridge
Venado	Venison

Aves (poultry)

Capón	Capon
Gallina	Hen
Oca	Goose
Pato	Duck
Pavo	Turkey
Pichón	Pigeon
Pollo	Chicken
Pularda	Pullet, small chicken

Pescados (fish)

Acedia	Plaice
Anguila	Eel
Angula	Elver
Arenque	Herring
Atún	Tuna
Bacalao	Salted Cod
Besugo	Sea bream
Bonito del Norte	White tuna
Boquerón	Anchovy (fresh)
Caballa	Mackerel

Cazón	Dogfish
Congro	Conger eel
Chanquete	Whitebait
Dorada	Sea Bream
Faneca	Whiting
Fletán	Halibut
Gallo	John Dory
Lamprea	Lamprey
Lenguado	Sole
Lubina	Sea-bass
Lucio	Pike
Merluza	Hake
Mero	Grouper
Pez espada	Swordfish
Rape	Angler fish
Reo	Ray trout
Rodaballo	Turbot
Rosada	Cod-like fish
Salmón	Salmon
Salmonete	Red mullet
Sardina	Sardine
Trucha	Trout

Mariscos (seafood)

Almeja	Clam
Berberecho	Cockle
Bigaro	Winkle
Bogavante	Lobster
Calamar	Squid
Camarón	Shrimp
Cangrejo	Crab
Carabinero	Scarlet Prawn
Centolla	Spider crab
Cigala	Crayfish
Gamba	Prawn

Langosta	Lobster
Langostino	King prawn
Mejillón	Mussel
Nécora	Fiddler crab
Ostra	Oyster
Percebe	Barnacle
Pulpo	Octopus
Vieira	Scallop

Postres/Dulces (desserts)

Almíbar	Syrup
Arroz con leche	Rice pudding
Bizcocho	Sponge cake
Bombones	Chocolates
Buñuelos	Fritters, doughnuts
Compota	Stewed fruit
Confitura	Jam
Crema	Cream
Flan	Crème caramel
Galletas	Biscuits
Helado	Ice cream
Hojaldre	Puff pastry
Jalea	Jelly
Mantecados	Shortcake
Merengue	Meringue
Milhojas	Vanilla slice
Nata	Cream
Natillas	Custard
Pastas	Fancy biscuits
Pasteles	Small cakes
Pastel de queso	Cheese cake
Rosquilla	Doughnuts
Sorbete	Sorbet, iced fruit
Tarta	Cake
Tarta de manzana	Apple tart

Torrijas	French toast
Tocino de cielo	Egg yolk & syrup
Tortas	Pie
Tortitas	Pancakes
Trufa	Truffle
Yemas	Candied egg yolks

Queso (cheese)

(Served before desserts or fruit.)

Manchego	Hard, ewe's milk
Queso de Bola	Round and mild
de Burgos	Soft and creamy
de Cabra	Goat
de Cabrales	Strong blue, goat's
Camerano	local white, goat's
de Cebrero	Veined, creamy, sharp
de Cincho	Hard, ewe's milk (also known as *camos*)
de Oveja	Sheep's milk
del país	Local cheese
Perilla	Firm, bland, cow's milk (also known as *teta*)
Roncal	Hand-pressed, salted and smoked, with sharp flavour, ewe's
San Simón	Firm, bland of Perilla
Ulloa	Soft, like Camembert
Villalón	Salty, ewe's milk.

Frutas (fruits)

Aguacate	Avocado
Albaricoque	Apricot
Castañas	Chestnuts
Cereza	Cherry
Chirimoya	Custard apple

Ciruela	Plum
Ciruela pasa	Prune
Coco	Coconut
Dátiles	Dates
Frambuesa	Raspberry
Fresa	Strawberry
Granada	Pomegranate
Grosellas	Redcurrants
Higo	Fig
Kiwi	Kiwi
Limón	Lemon
Macedonia	Fruit salad
Mandarina	Tangerine
Mango	Mango
Manzana	Apple
Melocotón	Peach
Melón	Melon
Membrillo	Quince
Moras	Blackberries
Naranja	Orange
Papaya	Paw-paw
Pasas de Corinto	Currants
Pasas de Malaga	Raisins
Pera	Pear
Piña	Pineapple
Plátano	Banana
Pomelo	Grapefruit
Sandía	Water-melon
Uvas	Grapes

Frutos Secos (nuts)

Almendra	Almond
Almendra garrapinada	Sugar almond
Avellana	Hazelnut
Cacahuete	Peanut

Castaña	Chestnut
Nuez	Walnut
Piñón	Pine-nut
Pistacho	Pistachio

Huevos/Tortillas (eggs/omelettes)

Tortilla espanola is the classic Spanish omelette made with potatoes, a little onion and lots of eggs, usually served cold and cut into wedges. It bears no resemblance to *Mexican tortilla*, and looks rather like a large cake, unlike *tortilla francesca*, which is a thin, plain omelette. There are many varieties and fillings including:

Tortilla de jamón	Ham omelette
Tortilla de queso	Cheese omelette
Tortilla gallega	Potato, ham, red peppers and peas

For the most delicious selection of tortillas, try the bar, Errjoxako Batzokja, 22 Mayor de Migueloa, Laguardia.

Huevos escalfados	Poached eggs
Huevos duros	Hard-boiled
Huevos a la flamenca	Baked with tomato, onion and small pieces of ham fried in oil, garnished with asparagus tips, red peppers or slices of spicy chorizo.
Huevos fritos	Fried eggs
Huevos al nido	'Egg in a nest' – egg yolks in small soft rolls, fried and then covered in the white of the egg.
Huevos pasados por agua	Soft-boiled
Huevos rellenos	Stuffed
Huevos revueltos	Scrambled
Huevos al trote	Boiled, stuffed with tuna and covered in mayonnaise

Revuelto de gambas   Scrambled eggs with prawns.

Bebidas (drinks)

Agua	Water
Agua con gas	Sparkling
Agua sin gas	Still water
Agua mineral	Mineral Water
Anís	Aniseed liqueur
Batido de leche	Milk shakes
Botella	Bottle
Café grande	Coffee (Large)
Café pequeño	Coffee (small)
Café capuccino	Capuccino
Café solo	Black coffee
Café con leche	White coffee
Café cortado	Coffee, with a dash of milk
Café descafeinado	Decaffeinated coffee
Carta de vinos	Wine list
Cava	Spanish sparkling wine, made by traditional method
Cerveza	Beer
(en botella)	Bottled
(caña)	Draught beer
Cerveza negra	Dark beer
(de barril)	Draught beer
(Sin alcohol)	Alcohol-free
Chocolate	Chocolate
(caliente/frió)	Hot/cold
Coñac	Cognac, Brandy
Copa	Glass
Cosecha	Vintage (year)
Cubalibre	Rum and coke
Dulce	Sweet
Espumoso	Sparkling
Fino	Light dry sherry
Gaseosa	Lemonade

Gin tonic	Gin and tonic
Granizado	Crushed ice drink
Hielo	Ice
Infusion	Herbal tea infusion
Jarra	Jug/pitcher/carafe
Jarrita	Small carafe
Jerez	Sherry
Jugo	Juice
Leche	Milk
Licor	Liqueur
Limonada	Lemonade
Manzanilla	Dry sherry (or comomile tea)
Naranjada	Orangeade
Oloroso	Strong dark sherry
Oporto	Port
Refrescos	Soft drinks
Ron	Rum
Sangría	Fruit, wine & brandy
Seco	Dry
Semi seco	Medium dry
Sidra	Cider
Sol y sombra	brandy and aniseed liqueur (literally means 'sun & shade' in Spanish)
Té	Tea
Té con leche	Tea with milk
Té con limón	Lemon tea
Té helados	Iced tea
Tinto de verano	Red wine, lemonade and ice
Tónica	Tonic
Vaso	Glass (also *copa*)
Vermút	Vermouth
Vino	Wine
Vino blanco	White wine
Vino de la casa	House wine
Vino de Jerez	Sherry

Vino del país	Local wine
Vino rosé	Rosé wine
Vino tinto	Red wine
Vodka	Vodka
Whisky (con soda)	Whisky (& soda)
Zumo	Juice
Zumo de tomate	Tomato juice
Zumo de naranja	Orange juice, normally freshly squeezed

Useful Phrases

Just a small portion	*Una ración pequeña*
Something light please	*Algo ligero, por favor*
Nothing more, thank you	*Nada mas, gracias*
The bill please	*La cuenta, por favor*

qué desea?	What would you like?
con gas o sin gas?	Fizzy or still (bottled water)?
grande o pequeño?	Large or small?
qué aproveche	enjoy your meal

APPENDIX D: CAMPSITES

La Rioja has a number of campsites, including those listed below. Prices are given as a guide only and are the daily rates levied in 1999 (exclusive of VAT). There are discounts for longer stays.

Bañares: 1,500 spaces. Open all year. Category 1 site situated off the Logroño to Burgos road in a thickly wooded area (✆ 941 322 804). Adult and children's swimming pools, bar, restaurant, cafeteria, supermarket, hot showers and tennis courts. Adults: 585 ptas (child: 535 ptas). Pitch: 2,320 ptas. Car: 585 ptas, Caravan: 585 ptas. Tent: 535 ptas. Motorhome: 985 ptas. Elec: 440 ptas.

Berceo: 320 spaces. Open all year. Category 1 site in a beautiful valley near the *Pilgrims' Way* and also on the **Monastery & Bodega Route** (see page 141) close to the San Lorenzo mountains (✆ 941 373 227). Attractive stone and wooden club house, spacious garden and wooded area. Adult: 500 ptas (child: 425 ptas). Pitch: 1,800 ptas. Car: 500 ptas. Caravan: 600 ptas. Tent: 450 ptas. Motorhome: 850 ptas. Elec: 375 ptas.

Castañares de Rioja: 1,100 spaces. Open all year. Category 1 site by the River Oja, situated at Km 85 on the Haro to Santa Domingo de la Calzada road (Spanish road signs often include a km figure, which is also given in addresses) between Casalarreina and Castañares (✆ 941 300 174). Adult and children's swimming pools, children's playground, mother and child room, children's playground, sports area and BBQ, supermarket, bar, restaurant, cafeteria, laundry/ironing room, **free** hot showers, **credit cards** accepted, etc. Adult: 690 ptas (child: 580 ptas). Car: 680 ptas. Motorhome: 1,400 ptas. Tent: 680 ptas. Elec: 425 ptas.

Fuenmayor: 500 spaces. Open all year. Category 1 site located around a mile from the town on Station Road on the banks of the River Ebro (✆ 941 450 330). Swimming pool, supermarket, games/TV room, children's playground, BBQ and tables, laundry service, but many statics. Adult: 500 ptas (child: 425ptas). Car: 500 ptas. Caravan: 500 ptas. Motorhome: 900 ptas. Tent: 500 ptas. Elec: 375 ptas.

Haro: 600 spaces. Open all year. Friendly owners. Category 2 site. Near the River Tirón within walking distance of the old town and its bodegas, *tapas* bars and shops (☎ 941 312 737). Tourist office is helpful and can provide a wealth of information. On site is a supermarket, laundry, hot showers, car washing, bar, cafeteria and adult and children's swimming pools. Adult: 495 ptas. (child: 390 ptas). Pitch: 990 ptas. Car: 495 ptas. Caravan: 495 ptas, Motorhome: 860 ptas. Elec: 310 ptas.

Logroño: 198 spaces. Open Easter week and during the summer. Category 2 site situated in the town by the River Ebro, near the municipal swimming pools (☎ 941 252 253). Supermarket, restaurant, bar, hot showers, laundry. Helpful tourist office in the centre at the tree-lined Espolón. Adult: 600 ptas (child: 550 ptas). Car: 600 ptas. Caravan: 750 ptas. Motorhome:1,200 ptas. Tent: 750 ptas. Elec. connection to each pitch.

Nájera: 154 spaces. Open 1st April to 1st October. Category 3 site in Nájera bordered by the Najerilla and Ebro rivers (☎ 941 360 102). Occupies a shady site with hot showers and a laundry. Adult: 575 ptas (child: 525 ptas). Car: 525 ptas. Caravan: 575 ptas. Motorhome: 975 ptas. Tent: 575 ptas. Elec. connections.

Navarette: 580 spaces. Open all year. Category 1 site on the *Pilgrims' Way* around a mile from the village on the road to Entrena (☎ 941 440 169). Swimming pool, tennis, mini-golf, children's playground, bar, cafe, supermarket, TV room, launderette, irons, car wash and baby changing facilities. Skiing and watersports are 40 minutes away. Adult: 585 ptas (child: 530 ptas). Car: 585 ptas. Caravan: 575 ptas. Motorhome: 975 ptas. Tent: 585 ptas. Elec. connections.

Villoslada de Cameros: 512 places. Open all year. Category 1 site in mountainous countryside near the village on the road to Lomos de Orio Hermitage (☎ 941 468 195). Cafe-bar, restaurant, supermarket, TV/video room, sports equipment rental shop, skiing and watersports, and a tourist information service. Adult: 465 ptas (child: 385 ptas). Car: 465 ptas. Caravan: 490 ptas. Motorhome: 855 ptas. Tent: 490 ptas. Elec: 415 ptas.

APPENDIX E: GLOSSARY

Abocado: Semi-dry.

Acero inoxidable: Stainless steel. Used to manufacture fermentation tanks as it allows greater control over the temperature and fermentation processes, which, coupled with modern computer controlled techniques, results in fruitier wines.

Acetic acid: Important volatile acid found in wine. Small amounts contribute to the palatable taste of wine, but larger quantities give a vinegary taste.

Acidity: Also known as ripe acidity, this is essential for the vitality and tanginess in a wine, although if there is too much the wine will taste too sharp.

Aftertaste: The flavour and aroma left in your mouth after wine has been swallowed that helps you assess how much you like it. Also known as the finish.

Aguardiente de Orujo: Spirit (fire-water!) produced from the distillation of the grape skins and pips left over from pressing and/or fermentation. This spirit is similar to the French marc and Italian grappa.

Alambrado: Fine wire mesh often used around the bottles of *reserva* and *gran reserva*, looking rather like a hair-net! Originally designed to prevent fraudulent replacement of the wine, but nowadays it is more for decoration. The wine waiter will neatly twist it out of the way.

Alcoholic strength: In general, less alcoholic wines come from the coolest climates as sunshine converts, by fermentation, the sugar in the grapes into ethyl alcohol. It is an important factor in giving wine its flavour and body.

Almacenista: A wine wholesaler who sells Riojan wines to bodegas.

Año: Year, e.g. of production.

Anti-oxidant: A chemical that stops wine or must from oxidising, e.g. sulphur dioxide or ascorbic acid (vitamin C).

Aroma: See *bouquet*.

Azufre: Sulphur.

Baked: Flavour associated with very hot sun on grapes. It can be controlled by harvesting at night and using modern cool-fermentation methods.

Balance: The harmony between the natural elements of acidity, alcohol, fruit and tannin.

Banderillas: Another name for bar-top *tapas*, usually served on a cocktail stick

Barrica: The French *barrique bordelaise* became Rioja's 225-litre *barrica bordelesa* used for ageing red wines, imparting tannins, colour and flavour. Unlike stainless steel, oak allows the wine to breathe and, depending on the age and type of oak, affects the maturing of the wine in a way that is still not fully understood.

Barrio: District (of a large town or city).

Bentonite: A fine clay containing a derivative of volcanic ash which is used as a 'fining agent' in wine processing to produce unclouded wine.

Big: Satisfying, strong, rounded, rich flavour.

Blanco: White. *Vino blanco* is white wine.

Blend: The majority of producers in Rioja blend wines using a mixture of their own grapes and bought-in grapes (growers 'fight' to buy grapes from the best growers) and they also buy-in wine to blend into their house style.

Blind tasting: All competitive tasting of wines is blind tasting, with the identity of the wine unknown to the taster.

BOB: Buyers Own Brand, e.g. a supermarkets own label wine. Supermarkets are increasingly using new names for their own label wines.

Bodega: A wine cellar, wine shop or a wine estate. When used on a wine label, it can also mean that the wine is estate bottled.

Body: Full bodied wines with plenty of alcohol and flavour.

Bordelesa: Another name for the 225-litre oak barrels (*barricas*) in which Rioja wine is aged.

Bota: A wine flask made from hide. Used in Haro at the annual *Battala dos Vinos* (Battle of the Wines) to spray copious amounts of wine at opponents! The modern successor is a fire extinguisher capable of shooting half a bottle of wine in five seconds!

Botella: Bottle.

Bottle-age: The length of time a wine spends in the bottle, as opposed to in a barrel. Bottle ageing has a mellowing effect on wine capable of being aged, e.g. Rioja *reservas* and *gran reservas*.

Bouquet: The complex smell produced by good maturing wine. A forceful aroma is a positive sign, in contrast to one that is weak and leaves little impression. The bouquet should smell clean – if it smells mouldy it can indicate wine aged in old barrels in a damp place or if 'sulphury' or 'tinny' it may be that the wine has not been made properly. Fruity or floral aromas indicate a young wine, while hints of vanilla or spices indicate the wine has probably been aged in wood. A smell of liquorice suggests older vines and is generally a sign of a good wine. In older, aged wines the complex bouquet may suggest leather, nutmeg, tobacco, nuts or even violets, and will be released as you swirl the wine around the glass. See **Tasting** on page 151.

Breathing: The action of air on wine after the bottle has been opened.

Breed: The balance of grapes, soil and skill used to produce quality wines.

Brown: Brown wine is too old to drink – except sherry or Madeira.

Cap: Literally the hat at the top of a vat during the fermentation period of red wines when the juice is in contact with the skins.

Capataz: Cellar master.

Capsule: The metal cap over a cork. This was originally lead and in some cases still is, but inorganic tin foil is now being used.

Carbonic maceration: Under this process the whole grape complete with its skin is passed into the fermentation tanks. Fermentation occurs inside the skin of the intact grapes under a 'blanket' of carbon dioxide gas, resulting in fruity, supple and low-tannin wines.

Carbon dioxide: The harmless gas produced during fermentation. It is also the bubbles in any fizzy drink, alcoholic or otherwise.

Cartilla: The form on which details of wine production are recorded, enabling the *Consejo Regulador* to keep a strict check on every Riojan wine produced, from grape-picking to eventual consumption.

Casa: House.

Casa del Vino: The official organisation (located in Laguardia) that assists winegrowers in the Alava province and encourages them to promote and market their own wines, rather than selling grapes or wines in bulk. It also provides technical expertise regarding viticulture and oenology, and has a modern laboratory for detailed analysis. There is also a small public wine museum.

Cask: See *barrica*. (An alternative word for a barrel.)

Catedral: The name used for the cellars at *Marqués de Riscal*, holding the bodega's oldest wines. (These cellars are usually called *cementerios*.)

Cava: Sparkling wine made by the champagne method (*método tradicional*), where the natural secondary fermentation takes place in the bottle. It is allowed to be made only in defined wine regions under strict regulations and is mainly produced in Penedes (Catalonia). However, La Rioja, Alava, Aragón, Navarra and Valencia are all regulated to produce Cava.

Cedarwood (cigar box): Used to describe the bouquet of a wine that has been in contact with oak.

Cementerio: Literally means graveyard, but the term is also used by most bodegas for the cellar containing their oldest wines. See also *catedral*.

Cesto: A grape-pickers basket with a capacity of 15 to 20kg (33 to 44lb) of grapes.

Chaptalisation: The addition of sugar to the grape juice at pressing time in order to increase the alcohol content.

Chiquito: A small measure of wine drunk in *tapas* bars, often served in a small tumbler.

Clarete: Not an official term, but now used in Rioja to describe light red or dark pink wine.

Clarificación: Fining. The process of the wine becoming clear and bright, rather than cloudy.

Classy: A vague term to indicate quality.

Clean: Free from defects.

Cloves: Part of the complex bouquet in wines produced using oak, caused by the toasting or burning of the inside of oak barrels.

Coarse: Not necessarily unpleasant wine, but rough and ready – certainly not fine.

Coconut: Another possible aroma found in the bouquet of wines that have been in contact with American oak.

Cold fermentation: Fermentation in stainless steel vats at controlled low temperatures.

Cold stabilisation: A rapid reduction in temperature to remove tartaric acid.

Colour: The colour of a wine contains vital clues during the tasting procedure. There are many tones of red with lively crimson, for example, indicating a young wine, while the older reds are a duller brick-red colour. Older wines also tend to lose colour pigments and become clearer and thinner in appearance. White wines can be almost clear, while young whites have greenish hues through to a yellow ochre colour, which is generally a sign that the wine may have suffered from oxidation.

Comporta: A large wooden tub holding 80 to 120kg (176 to 265lb) of grapes.

Consejo Regulador: The strict official organisation (based in Logroño) established to control, defend and promote the Rioja *Denominación de Origen.*

Contara: A capacity of 16 litres.

Coop/Cooperativa: A wine co-operative.

Corcho: Cork.

Corked: The smell of a bottle with a mouldy cork.

Corquete: An implement used to pick grapes that is similar to a small curved sickle.

Cortacápsulas: Foil-cutter.

Cosecha: Harvest, vintage or crop, e.g. Cosecha 1994.

Cosechero: A small winegrower (small scale – not a small man!).

Cosecheros wine: Young, un-aged quaffing wine from the current year that is worth trying when in Rioja. It is inexpensive and fruity and very popular in Rioja.

Criado y embotellado por . . : Grown and bottled by . .

Crianza: Indicates that a wine is in its third year when released for sale and at least two years old with one year aged in oak. *Sin crianza* means un-oaked, as in young (*joven*) wines.

Cuerpo: Body.

CVC (Conjunto Varias Cosechas): A blend of various vintages. The back-label on the wine bottle is green. Some 15 per cent of Rioja's wine production is CVC.

Degustación: Tasting.

Degustador: Taster.

Denominación de Origen (DO): The official qualification of a Spanish wine of an approved type and standard from a specific region.

Denominación de Origen Calificada (DOCa): The coveted classification for wines of the highest quality. Riojan wines are the only wines in Spain to qualify for this honour (since 1991).

Deposit: Natural sediment normally consisting of tartaric acid crystals in white wine, which are harmless. The sediment from red wines and vintage port should be carefully decanted off just before drinking. Use a light (candle or torch) shining underneath the neck of the bottle as the wine is slowly and carefully poured out, to check when the sediment appears. Do not throw away this sediment, but save it and add it to soup or stews – scrummy!

Depósito: A closed wooden vat or tank used for storing or fermenting wine.

Depth: Fills your mouth with flavour – present in all good wine.

DO: See *Denominación de Origen*.

Dulce: Sweet.

Elaboración: Wine making and maturation.

Elaborado y añejado por . . : Made and aged by . .

Elegant: Indefinable but obvious.

Embotellado por . . . : Bottled for . . .

Enología: Oenology. The science of wine and wine-making.

Enológico: Oenologist, usually with a university degree.

En vaso: The typical way of pruning in Rioja, so-called because after pruning the vines look like a wine glass (a *vaso* is a glass in Spanish). This method minimises the work necessary to maintain vines and protects them from strong winds and excess sun, but it also makes mechanical harvesting impossible.

En espaldera: The newer style of training vines along wires or trellising. Grapes are more open to the sun and mechanical harvesting is possible.

Espumoso: Sparkling.

Estación de Viticultura y Enología: The government laboratory in Haro (founded in 1902) that works in conjunction with the *Consejo Regulador*. Their main task is the analysis of wines to ensure that they conform to the standards of the *reglamento* (rules), although research is also carried out on all aspects of the production of Riojan wines. The wine museum is well worth a visit.

Ethyl Alcohol: This is produced in wine-making and is the result of the fermentation of grape juice by yeast enzymes, with the release of carbon dioxide gas.

Etiqueta: Label.

Fermentación alcóholica: The process whereby sugar in grape juice is changed by fermentation into alcohol and carbon dioxide gas.

Fermentación maloláctica: A natural process of converting tart malic acid into softer lactic acid.

Filtration: The process of pumping wine through different filters to remove solids, which may also filter out the flavour.

Finesse: The fine-ness or delicacy of a wine.

Fining: The clarification (*clarificación*) of wine immediately after fermentation using egg whites, bentonite (a clay which swells as it absorbs water, originally formed by the decomposition of volcanic ash), gelatine and even dried blood, resulting in the solids falling out of wine. Bovine Spongiform Encephalopathy (BSE), more commonly know as 'mad cow disease', has reduced the practice of using blood.

Finish: The finish of a wine is the last flavour remaining on the palate. The better the wine, the longer the finish, with length indicating how long the finish lasts!

Fruity: Refers to the body and richness of wine made from good ripe grapes.

Gran Reserva: Wines chosen from an exceptional vintage or a blend of *reservas* capable of further ageing in oak. The minimum age is five years, with at least two years in oak.

These wines should last for 15 to 20 years, depending on how they have been stored, although there are exceptions.

Grapes: Red grapes are used to produce red and rosé wines, although some sparkling rosé is made by blending red and white wines. White grapes produce white wines.

Grub: Dig out and remove vines.

Grupo de Exportadores de Vinos Rioja: The group of Rioja wine exporters, to which all exporting Rioja bodegas must belong.

Hard: In wine terminology, this indicates an uncompromising lack of subtlety and softness, which is sometimes improved with ageing.

Hectare: The equivalent of 2.47 acres or 10,000 square metres.

Inert gas: Used to prevent oxidation by being pumped into the space above wine in its container. Nitrogen gas is an example.

Injerto: Vine graft.

Irrigation: The irrigation of vines is a matter of heated debate and vehemently opposed by traditionalists, but it is creeping into areas that have not used it before. The narrow pipes must provide the optimum amount of moisture – too much will produce thin wine.

Joven: Young, un-oaked wine generally intended to be drunk within the year following the harvest (although there are exceptions) – after two years it can be a lottery. It is relatively low in alcohol and better when fermented at low temperatures to enhance the fruit and bouquet.

Lees: Another term for the sediment in a wine.

Legs: Refers to the 'tears' that are deposited on the side of a glass after you have swirled the wine around, indicating quality and the strength of the alcohol content. With some pleasurable practice you can become adept at estimating the alcoholic strength. There is a divergence of opinion on whether it is glycerine or not – keep swirling!

Levadura: Yeast.

Licoroso: Strong, i.e. high in alcohol.

Light: Can be a term of approval with some white wines, but the opposite with reds, suggesting a lack of body, colour and alcohol.

Long: Describes the finish of a wine and is the aftertaste.

Maceration: The process of fermenting grape juice remaining in contact with the grape skins. With red wines, maceration usually takes several days and with rosés it can be up to 36 hours, although it may not take place at all with white wines.

Maceration carbonic: Whole grapes are fermented intact in sealed vats under a blanket of carbon dioxide gas, resulting in light, fruity wines, usually intended to be drunk young.

Madera: Wood.

Madera Nueva: New wood, usually oak (*roble*), imparting intense and distinctive flavours.

Maderised: Means that the wine has been exposed to heat and air and deteriorated, giving an unpleasant taste. The wine also looks darker-coloured and unappetising. The wine should be rejected or returned to where it was purchased – unless of course it has been maderised deliberately as in the case of Madeira or the Spanish *rancio*, a nutty flavoured wine. See also **Chapter 5** (Enjoying Wine).

Malolactic fermentation: The secondary, non-alcoholic fermentation that converts the malic acid present in wine into lactic acid and carbon dioxide gas. It results in a more stable wine with less acidity, and although hardly ever used for white and rosé Riojas, it is essential for the reds.

Meaty: Suggests that a wine has enough body to chew it!

Mesón: Describes a meeting or eating place, a bit like a British country pub.

Método tradicional: Traditional method. This term replaced the French *méthode champenoise* from 31st August 1994 and describes the method of making Cava.

Must: The newly pressed juice of grapes ready for fermentation.

Musty: An unpleasant smell, probably from a rotten stave in a barrel.

Nitrogen: Used to protect wine from oxidisation in some cellars by covering the vats with a blanket of nitrogen gas. It is used to keep the better wines fresh in some wine bars and restaurants where wine is sold by the glass. This is better than a vacuum wine saver, which can leech out (remove) the bouquet of the wine.

Noble: The combination of breed, maturity and body in a fine wine.

Nose: Not only the protuberance on your face, sometimes variously coloured, but also the means of 'smelling tastes'. See also *bouquet* and **Chapter 5** (Enjoying Wine).

Oak: Either French or American, each of which have similar, but also different, characteristics. It imparts colour, flavour and tannins and, unlike stainless steel or lined cement, allows wine to breathe. French oak barrels cost around twice as much as American barrels, the wood being imported from France and Spanish coopers making the barrels. See also **Oak** on page 28.

Oenology (pronounced 'eenology'): The science of wine production that is responsible for overall consistency and standards, resulting in marked improvements in many wine regions in recent years.

Origen: Wine from the last vintage that has not undergone the *crianza* process.

Oxidación: Oxidation. *Oxidado* is an oxidised wine.

Oxidised: See 'maderised' and 'wine faults'.

Phenolics: A varied group of organic compounds found mainly in skins, stems, and in the case of grapes, seeds also. Precipitated, they form an important part of a wine's sediment and play a considerable role in the ageing of wines. Phenolics in red wine reduce the amount of cholesterol deposited in the arteries making heart attacks less likely. Phenolics include anthocyans, *tannins* and some flavour compounds.

Phylloxera: This vine pest not only produced notable changes in wine production, but caused panic in Western Europe as wine growers grubbed out vineyards and abandoned land as the aphid spread. This tiny louse loves to feed on vine roots and, not surprisingly, the vines die, as they did in the 19th century literally in front of the panic-stricken growers' eyes. This happened first in France and then through most wine regions of the world, with only vines shown to be resistant to phylloxera surviving, such as certain native American species and vines growing in very dry or sandy areas such as Chile.

One of the results of this devastation was the movement of *vignerons* from Bordeaux to Rioja bringing with them their expertise and Cabernet Sauvignon grapes. (Although the *Consejo Regulador* approves only seven grape varieties, Cabernet Sauvignon has a special dispensation.) After much experimentation and heartache it was found that phylloxera could be combated by grafting *vinifera* vines on to American root-stock, a method still used today on almost 90 per cent of the world's wine producing vines.

Porrón: A flask with an long neck or spout that may be made of wood, leather or glass. An accomplished user projects a jet of wine into his mouth, while the unskilled pour it all over their clothes!

Prensa: Press.

Pressing: The process of extracting the juice from grapes by treading them underfoot, the traditional method, or with pneumatic presses.

Probador: A wine-tasting room.

Provir: A group of 15 small to medium, quality-conscious Riojan wine producers who have banded together for publicity purposes and who are eager to show you around their bodegas. These are marked *Provir* after the bodega's name in **Chapter 2** (Rioja's Bodegas).

Pruning: A vital and skilled job done during the winter. With a few skilful snips of the secateurs, the vines are shaped and the number of bunches of grapes determined for the next season. In cooler climes where heat and sunlight to ripen the grapes are more limited, it is the primary method of influencing the yield (the hectolitres of wine per hectare of vineyard).

Racking: The transference of wine (to clear it) from one barrel to another in order to leave the lees behind. In some bodegas the last of the sedimented wine is left to clear and given to the cellar workers. It is considered a fault in Rioja if wines need to be decanted before drinking.

Reserva: Wines aged for a minimum of three years with at least one year in oak. As a general rule, they should be good for 8 to 12 years, but this varies and depends on the grapes, the method used to make the wine, the house style and how the wine has been stored.

Residual sugar: The natural grape sugar left in the wine after fermentation.

Retrogusto: The finish after tasting a wine.

Río: River.

Roble: Oak from trees with the genus Quercus Ruber.

Rosado: Rosé.

Rough: Cheap, badly made wine.

Sacacorchos: Corkscrew.

Sangría: A long, cold, red wine cup, traditionally made with fizzy lemonade, citrus fruits, brandy and ice.

Sarmiento: Vine shoot. Meats are often cooked over vine shoots (*al sarmiento*).

Seco: Dry – semi-seco is semi-dry.

Semi-dulce: Semi-sweet.

Sense of smell: Man's sense of smell is some 10,000 times more acute than his sense of taste and therefore it is the single most important factor in wine tasting.

Short: Not surprisingly, this is the opposite of long when applied to wine! It is a critical term that indicates a wine has no real 'finish'. See also *length* and *finish*.

Sin Crianza: Mainly young wines having little or no maturation in barrel, but the term can also be used for older wines made without ageing in barrels. Most white Riojan wines are *sin crianza*.

Single Estate Wines: A single vineyard wine produced entirely from grapes grown within an estate's (bodega's) own vineyards.

Slurp: The only polite time to make this noise is when tasting wine. You suck in air together with the wine to release the bouquet through the nostrils and soft palate into the upper part of the nasal cavity. The moisture in the cavity dissolves these vapours that go to the olfactory lobe in the brain (the nearby temporal lobe is the memory bank). The analysis takes place in the parietal lobe and finally the wine is judged in the frontal lobe. The sense of smell has a wonderful ability to awaken memories!

Sociedad Anónima (SA): A public limited company.

Socio: A member of a wine-growing co-operative. The *socio* sells his crop to the co-operative to be made into wine.

Soft: Used to describe a wine that is easy on the palate due to residual sugar.

Soil: A vineyard's soil is one of the main factors that determine a wine's characteristics.

Sommelier: A wine waiter or wine steward. The master *sommelier* qualification is highly respected throughout the world.

Stalk: A green woody smell from an under-ripe vintage.

Storage: Should be free from vibration, strong light and strong smells and without large variations in temperature.

Sugars: These are stored in the woody trunk of the vine. An old vine bears less fruit, but has a greater concentration of sugars. See also *vines*.

Sulphur Dioxide and Sulphur: Widely used in vineyards to protect against the fungus oidium. Sulphur tablets are burnt inside wooden barrels to eradicate unwanted wild yeasts. Sulphur dioxide is also used in the space in bottles between the wine and the cork to prevent oxidisation. As some asthmatics react badly to it, a warning is required on wine labels in some countries, e.g. the USA.

Tannins: Found mainly in red wines and come from the skins, seeds and stalks of dark red grapes. All red wines destined for ageing need tannins, but this must be counterbalanced with fruit, the control of which is one of the winemaker's most important tasks. Tannins are also preservative *Phenolics*.

Tapas: Traditional Spanish bar snacks. The small sample is a *porción* or *pincho* and is a good way of trying a selection of *tapas*, which can be followed with a larger helping (*ración*) of those you prefer.

Taste: As usual, first impressions *do* count! Is the wine smooth, intense, chewy or so full flavoured that it suggests you could almost chew it? If there is lots of tannin it will be full flavoured but astringent, and dry your mouth rather unpleasantly, suggesting that it may need time to mellow. If well matured, it will be rounded and you will taste it all around your mouth in contrast to a less-balanced wine, which will taste different depending on which part of the tongue it comes into contact with. A burning taste indicates an excess of alcohol, while the aftertaste should be lengthy and leave a distinct memory, rather than a fleeting one. If you have a cold you will lose your sense of taste and you should never smoke while tasting wine.

Tartaric acid: The harmless white crystals sometimes found in white wine, and – surprise, surprise – red-coloured crystals in red wine. They can be removed in the winemaking process by a rapid reduction in temperature to crystallise them out.

Tears: See *legs*.

Terroir: Literally earth, indicating an earthy taste.

Tinaja: Earthenware.

Tinto: Spanish for red (but only when used for wine, otherwise red is *rojo*), e.g. *vino tinto* is red wine.

Toasted: The charring inside oak barrels made by the cooper. It also describes the taste imparted by this process (see *tonelería* below).

Tonelería: Where the barrels are made and stored for sale, such as Murúa of Logroño, a family business founded in 1920. A lot of the manual work, such as sawing and planing is no longer labour intensive, but the actual production of the barrel is still a skilled craft performed by hand. The well-seasoned wood is mainly American oak, but also French from Allier, Limousin, Tronçais or Vosges. Each barrel (*barrica*) requires 27 to 30 shaped staves 95cm in length, which are held together by eight galvanised hoops. When the first hoops are positioned to hold the barrel together at one end, the open staves are heated and scorched to make them flexible and then winched together so that more hoops can be hammered down over the belly. The heads and bottoms are added, each consisting of five to seven boards, and made watertight by the addition of strips of reed. The amount of scorching or toasting of the inside of the barrel influences the character and taste of the wine.

Tonelero: A cooper.

Trasiega: Racking, which involves the transfer of wine off its lees (sediment) into a clean barrel.

Uva: Grape.

Vanilla: A distinctive taste and smell imparted to wine by oak barrels.

Vat: A large storage tank or barrel made of wood, stainless steel, fibre-glass or even concrete. (Also a tax which makes the difference between affordable and too expensive!)

VCPRD: Used on wine labels within the European Union to indicate high quality wines produced in a given area.

Vendimia: Harvest or vintage.

Vid: Vine.

Viejo: Old or aged.

Viña or viñedo: Single vineyard, but on a label the term may be used loosely and does not necessarily mean that the wine originates from a particular vineyard.

Vines: Can be 40, 50 or even 60 years old. Old vines, if treated correctly, will produce powerful wines with a hint of liquorice. Old wines also produce less fruit, have a greater concentration of sugars. Young or recently planted vines need four or five years before the fruit is of an acceptable quality.

Vinifera: In Europe and the Middle East, vitis vinifera or simply vinifera, is the one and only native vine species, from which almost all of the world's most famous wines are made. Within each species there are thousands of different varieties, of which Chardonnay and Cabernet Sauvignon are two of the best known.

Vinification: The production of wine from pressing to its final ageing.

Vino: Wine.

Vino añejo: Mellow, mature wine.

Vino del año: New wine, wine of the year, for early drinking.

Vino de la casa: House wine.

Vino corriente/peleón: Ordinary, plonk!

Vino de cosechero (del año/sin crianza): Traditional Riojan fermentation where uncrushed grapes produce lighter, fruity un-oaked wine. Popular in Rioja and intended to be drunk young.

Vino de Mesa: Ordinary table wine as opposed to *Vino de la Tierra* or *DO*.

Vino de Pago: Wine made from grapes from a particular vineyard, aged and bottled on the estate, i.e. estate bottled.

Vino de la Tierra: A new Spanish designation similar to the French *vin de pays*.

Vinolento: Boozy, fond of the bottle!

Vintage: The year of the harvest (the time of harvesting varies depending on the region and the country).

Viticultura: Viticulture. The cultivation of vines for the production of wine. The location of the vineyard, the vine variety or varieties, how the vines are grown and how the wine is made, all influence the resulting wine.

Viticultor: Winegrower.

Well-balanced: Good proportions of acid, alcohol and flavours.

Yeasts: These ferment the sugars in grapes to produce ethyl alcohol and are present in traditional wine-growing areas in the air and on grape skins. Problems may arise with harmful 'wild yeasts' that can affect the fermentation.

Yeast Research: This is being done on the construction of yeast in order to produce more glycerol and less acetic acid to help improve wine quality. Alcohol and glycerol are the main by-products of fermentation, with glycerol giving sweetness and fullness. Scientists have modified the yeast 'sacchoromyces cerevisiae' by boosting the gene responsible for producing the enzyme that determines the amount of glycerol, and removing the gene responsible for acetic acid. The new strains produce two to three times as much glycerol and fermentation takes place more quickly, thus saving time and money. This should be particularly beneficial in colder areas, helping to make wines with greater body, but these industrial strains require large-scale testing to prove that they work in practice with no harmful side-effects. (Let's hope we don't develop two heads!)

Yield: The maximum yield permitted varies with the country and the area, and is restricted in order to protect quality. For example, in Rioja it is 6,500kg (14,329lb) per hectare for red grapes and 9,000kg (19,841lb) per hectare for white grapes.

APPENDIX F: VINTAGES

The Regulating Council (*Consejo Regulador*) declares (in May) one of the following five vintage classifications for the previous year's grape harvest:

E	*Excelente*	Excellent
MB	*Muy Buena*	Very good
B	*Buena*	Good
N	*Normal*	Normal
M	*Mediana*	Average

The following vintages have been declared since 1930:

1930	M	1931	MB	1932	N	1933	N
1934	E	1935	MB	1936	N	1937	N
1938	M	1939	N	1940	N	1941	B
1942	MB	1943	B	1944	B	1945	N
1946	N	1947	MB	1948	E	1949	MB
1950	N	1951	N	1952	E	1953	M
1954	B	1955	E	1956	B	1957	N
1958	E	1959	MB	1960	B	1961	B
1962	MB	1963	N	1964	E	1965	M
1966	N	1967	N	1968	MB	1969	N
1970	MB	1971	M	1972	M	1973	B
1974	B	1975	MB	1976	B	1977	N
1978	MB	1979	N	1980	B	1981	MB
1982	E	1983	B	1984	N	1985	B
1986	B	1987	MB	1988	B	1989	B
1990	B	1991	MB	1992	B	1993	B
1994	E	1995	E	1996	MB	1997	B
1998	MB						

APPENDIX G: BASQUE LANGUAGE

Spanish is the official language of La Rioja region, but in the Basque Country (*País Vasco, Euskadi*), Basque is also an official language. Although everybody speaks Spanish, it is useful to know a few words of Basque (*Euskera*), particularly those used on official signs (such as road signs), which are often bilingual.

BASQUE	SPANISH	ENGLISH
Agur	Adiós	Goodbye
Aireportua	Aeropuerto	Airport
Aparkalekua	Aparcamiento	Parking
Bai	Sí	Yes
Donostia	San Sebastián	San Sebastian
Egunon	Buenos días	Good morning
Eguna	Día	Day
*Ertzaintzal**	Policía Autónoma	Autonomous Police
Euskadi	País Vasco	Basque Country
Ez	No	No
Gabon	Buenas noches	Good night
Gasteiz	Vitoria	Vitoria
Hotela	Hotel	Hotel
Jatetxea	Restaurante	Restaurant
Kaixo	Hola	Hello
Mesedez	Por Favor	Please
Ongi etorri	Bienvenido	Welcome
Turismo Bulegoa	Oficina de Turismo	Tourist Office
Udaletxea	Ayuntamiento	Town Hall
Udaltzaingoa#	Policía Municipal	Municipal Police

* Red & Blue uniform, red beret (duties include public order, traffic control, municipal services).

Blue Uniform (local and municipal services). The National Police, responsible for public order also wear blue uniforms, while the Civil Guard (Guardia Civil) have green uniforms and are responsible for ports and airports.

APPENDIX H: USEFUL INFORMATION

Airlines

British Airways (℡ UK 0345-222111) London (Heathrow) to Bilbao.
Easyjet (℡ UK 0870-600 0000, 🖳 www.easyjet.com).
GO (℡ UK 0845-605 4321, 🖳 www.go-fly.com), London (Stanstead) to Bilbao.
Iberia (℡ UK 0207-830 0011) London (Heathrow) to Bilbao.
Spanish Travel Services (℡ UK 0207- 387 5337).

Banks

Business hours are generally from 8.30am to 2pm from Mondays to Fridays (savings banks have extended hours on certain days from 4pm to 5.30pm) and on Saturdays from 9am to 1pm from October to May. Most credit cards are accepted for cash advances.

Car Hire

Avis (℡ UK 0990-900500).
Budget (℡ UK 0800-181181).
Hertz (℡ UK 0990-996699).

Emergencies

Emergency numbers (*Servicios de Urgencia*) are listed at the front of telephone directories (white and yellow pages) and include 062 (*Guardia Civil*), 091 (municipal police) and 112 (*Protección Civil* and SOS Rioja). The general emergency number is 088 in the Basque Country. The *Ertzaintza* (autonomous Basque police) respond to all emergency calls such as accident, fire and other emergencies.

Ferry Companies

Brittany Ferries (UK Reservations & Enquiries, ℡ UK 0990-360 360, 🖳 www.brittany-ferries.com) operate scheduled services from Plymouth or Portsmouth (depending on the time of the year) to Santander. Twice weekly crossing.

Ferrysavers (℞ UK 0700-233 7743) For competitive prices on all routes.

Hoverspeed (℞ UK 0870-524 0241).

P&O (Portsmouth Reservations, ℞ UK 0870-242 4999, 🖳 www.poef.com or www.poportsmouth.com) operate scheduled services from Portsmouth to Bilbao, twice weekly.

P&O Stena (℞ UK 0870-600 0600). Dover to Calais.

SeaFrance (℞ UK 0870-571 1711).

Eurotunnel (℞ UK 0870-535 3535).

Fishing

Only annual permits are issued in La Rioja and the procedure is time consuming. Incidentally, all fish landed must be thrown back (they only allow 'fishing without death'!).

Golf

There is only one golf club in the region, *Golf Club of Larrabea* (18 holes, Par 72, ℞ 945 465 844, 🖷 945 465 725), which is not in the La Rioja region itself, but near Vitoria, around one hour by car from Logroño.

Hot Air Balloon Flights

Hot air balloon flights are available from Arcoiris (℞ 608 976 061, 🖷 941 304 076) in Haro who organise flights of around one-hour's duration for a minimum of two people, including complimentary wine and a certificate (to show that you have flown in a balloon, not drunk Rioja!). The cost in 1999 was 20,000 ptas per person.

Marketing Agency – Red Rioja

This is not a wine, but the name of an extremely helpful specialist company in Logroño that provides comprehensive information about Rioja. They can provide wine contacts and organise package tours for visitors. Contact Concha Penaranda,

Villamediana 9–2 D, 26003 Logroño (℘ 941 271 203, 📠 941 271 205, ✉ info@redrioja.com, 💻 www.redrioja.com).

Post Offices

Post offices in La Rioja are usually open from 8.30am to 8.30pm on weekdays and from 9.30am to 2pm on Saturdays. In summer there may be limited working hours in some post offices. Stamps can also be purchased from tobacconists (*estancos*).

Tour Operators

Arblaster & Clarke Wine Tours (℘ 0173-089 3344, 📠 01730-892888, ✉ sales@winetours.co.uk, 💻 www.winetours. co.uk).

Krossover Links (27 Playa de Sitges, Punta Galea, 28230 Las Rozas, Madrid, ℘ 916 303 070, 📠 916 302 198, ✉ emusique@mad.servicom.es) organise tailor-made, 3-day (two nights), English-speaking, escorted tours for groups of 20 people. They include a 4-star, air-conditioned hotel, visits to two bodegas with a tasting commentary and gastronomic meal, and a panoramic drive through vineyards and medieval villages. Arrival and departure is from Bilbao Airport.

Mundi Color (℘ 0207-828 6021) offer city breaks in Spain.

Tanglewood Wine Tours (℘ 01932-348720, 📠 01932-350861).

Winetrail (℘ 01306-712111, 📠 01306-713504, ✉ sales@ winetrails.co.uk, 💻 www.winetrails.co.uk).

Tourist Offices

Tourist Offices in Rioja are extremely helpful and at least one of the staff can speak English. They can provide lists of hotels, apartments/villas to let, restaurants, maps, etc. and you can telephone, fax or e-mail offices for information. In summer, they usually open from 10am to 2pm and from 4.30pm to 7.30pm, Mondays to Saturdays, and from 10am to 2pm on Sundays and public holidays. There are restricted opening times in winter, normally posted on doors, which vary depending on the particular office.

Alfaro	✆ 941 180 032, 📠 941 183 893
Arnedillo	✆/📠 941 394 226, ✉ oficina@valcicados.es, 🖥 www.valcicados.es
Arnedo	✆ 941 383 988, 📠 941 383 164, ✉ ayto.amedo@lgr.servicom.es
Calahorra	✆/📠 941 146 398, 🖥 www.supervia.com/calaguris
Ezcaray	✆/📠 941 427 184
Haro	✆ 941 303 366, 📠 941 303 366, ✉ riojalta@arrakis.es, 🖥 www.arrakis.es/-rioalta. (N.B. The door is off-putting and the office is dark, making it appear to be closed!)
Logroño	✆ 941 260 665, 📠 941 256 045
Nájera	✆/📠 941 360 041
Pradillo	✆/📠 941 462 147, ✉ altura@arrakis.es, 🖥 www.cmrioja.es/turismo/altura.html
San Millán de la Cogolla	✆/📠 941 373 259
Santo Domingo de la Calzada	✆/📠 941 341 230, ✉ santodomingo@rioja.org, 🖥 www.rioja.org

Travel Agents

Viajes Román Paladino (17-19 Calle Chile, Logroño (✆ 941 201 172, or 📠 941 214 654) is a small, independent travel agency in Logroño owned by the charming Carmen Merino Lozano, who will not only help you with all your travel needs, but is also a fund of knowledge on the history of Rioja. She will even take you on an escorted tour of historic Logroño during her two-hour lunch break (by appointment).

Useful Websites

Tourism:

www.arrakis.es/-rialta
www.compostela2000.com
www.larioja.com./turismo
www.sanmillan.com

Travel:

www.eurotunnel.com
www.ferrysavers.co.uk
www.iti.fr (French route planner)
www.redrioja.com
www.seafrance.com

Wine:

www.berry-bros.co.uk
www.bordeauxdirect.co.uk
www.chateauonline.co.uk
www.enjoyment.co.uk
www.oddbins.co.uk
www.orgasmicwines.com
www.purewine.co.uk
www.redrioja.com
www.tanglewoodwine.com (including wine storage cabinets)
www.vine2wine.com
www.winewinewine.co.uk
www.zoom.co.uk

Note: You can find others using 'search engines' such as Yahoo and Altavista.

Wine Shops (*bodegas*)

Briñas

El Portal de la Rioja (on the Logroño to Vitoria road at km39). They also have a small museum.

Fuenmayor

Vinoteca Cuchi (next to their restaurant).

Haro:

Comercial Vinícola Riojana/La Hermandad Vinícola (7 Calle Santo Tomás, ☎ 941 303 156, 📠 941 312 828).

Selección Vinos de Rioja (Isabel Gutiérrez Ortiz, 5 Plaza de la Paz).

Juan González Muga (17 Calle Santo Tomás and 2 Calle Castillo).

La Catedral de los Vinos (4, C/Santo Tomás).

Laguardia

La Vinoteca (1 Plaza Mayor).

Logroño

La Catedral del Vino (25 Calle Portalis – in front of the Cathedral).

Helen Rioja (5-7 Calle Marqués de Murrieta).

Palacio del Vino (136-142 Avenida de Burgos – on the outskirts).

Viños de Rioja (41 Pl. San Augustin).

All the above shops also stock a selection of local speciality foods, conveniently packed in tins for transportation. These include *aspárragos blancos* (white, thick asparagus), *pimientos de piquillo* (piquant red peppers), olive oil, wine vinegars and various other treats such as unusual patés.

INDEX

C

E

ORDER FORM – ALIEN'S/BUYING A HOME

Qty.	Title	Price (incl. p&p)			Total
		UK	**Euro.**	**World**	
	The Alien's Guide to America	Winter 2000-01			
	The Alien's Guide to Britain	£5.95	£6.95	£8.45	
	The Alien's Guide to France	£5.95	£6.95	£8.45	
	Buying a Home in Abroad	£11.45	£12.95	£14.95	
	Buying a Home in Britain	£11.45	£12.95	£14.95	
	Buying a Home in Florida	£11.45	£12.95	£14.95	
	Buying a Home in France	£11.45	£12.95	£14.95	
	Buying a Home Greece/Cyprus	£11.45	£12.95	£14.95	
	Buying a Home in Ireland	£11.45	£12.95	£14.95	
	Buying a Home in Italy	£11.45	£12.95	£14.95	
	Buying a Home in Portugal	£11.45	£12.95	£14.95	
	Buying a Home in Spain	£11.45	£12.95	£14.95	
	Rioja and its Wines	£11.45	£12.95	£14.95	
				Total	

Order your copies today by phone, fax, mail or e-mail from Survival Books, PO Box 146, Wetherby, West Yorks. LS23 6XZ, United Kingdom (☎/🖷 +44-1937-843523, ✉ orders@survivalbooks.net, 🖥 www.survivalbooks. net). If you aren't entirely satisfied, simply return them to us within 14 days for a full and unconditional refund.

Cheque enclosed/please charge my Delta/Mastercard/Switch/Visa card

Card No.   _ _ _ _   _ _ _ _   _ _ _ _   _ _ _ _

Expiry date _____ Issue No. (Switch only) _____

Signature _____ **Tel. No.** _____

NAME _____

ADDRESS _____

_____

ORDER FORM – LIVING AND WORKING

Qty.	Title	Price (incl. p&p)			Total
		UK	**Euro.**	**World**	
	Living & Working in Abroad	Winter 2000-01			
	Living & Working in America	£14.95	£16.95	£20.45	
	Living & Working in Australia	£14.95	£16.95	£20.45	
	Living & Working in Britain	£14.95	£16.95	£20.45	
	Living & Working in Canada	£14.95	£16.95	£20.45	
	Living & Working in France	£14.95	£16.95	£20.45	
	Living & Working in Germany	Summer 2000			
	Living & Working in Italy	Autumn 2000			
	Living & Working in London	£11.45	£12.95	£14.95	
	Living & Working in N.Z.	£14.95	£16.95	£20.45	
	Living & Working in Spain	£14.95	£16.95	£20.45	
	Living & Working in Switz.	£14.95	£16.95	£20.45	
				Total	

Order your copies today by phone, fax, mail or e-mail from Survival Books, PO Box 146, Wetherby, West Yorks. LS23 6XZ, United Kingdom (☎/🖷 +44-1937-843523, ✉ orders@survivalbooks.net, 🖥 www.survivalbooks. net). If you aren't entirely satisfied, simply return them to us within 14 days for a full and unconditional refund.

Cheque enclosed/please charge my Delta/Mastercard/Switch/Visa card

Card No. _ _ _ _   _ _ _ _   _ _ _ _   _ _ _ _

Expiry date _____ Issue No. (Switch only) _____

Signature _____ **Tel. No.** _____

NAME _____

ADDRESS _____

_____

LIVING AND WORKING IN SPAIN

Living and Working in Spain is essential reading for anyone planning to spend some time there including holiday-home owners, retirees, visitors, business people, migrants, students and even extraterrestrials! It's packed with over 400 pages of important and useful information designed to help you **avoid costly mistakes and save both time and money.** Topics covered include how to:

- find a job with a good salary
- obtain a residence permit
- avoid and overcome problems
- find your dream home
- get the best education
- make the best use of public transport
- endure motoring in Spain
- obtain the best health treatment
- stretch your pesetas (euros) further
- make the most of your leisure time
- enjoy the Spanish sporting life
- find the best shopping bargains
- insure yourself against most things
- use the post office and telephones
- do numerous other things

Living and Working in Spain is the most comprehensive and up-to-date source of practical information available about everyday life in Spain. It isn't, however, a boring text book, but an interesting and entertaining guide written in a highly readable style.

Buy this book and discover what it's <u>really</u> like to live and work in Spain.

Order your copies today by phone, fax, mail or e-mail from Survival Books, PO Box 146, Wetherby, West Yorks. LS23 6XZ, United Kingdom (☎/🖷 +44-1937-843523, ✉ orders@ survivalbooks.net, 🖳 www.survivalbooks.net).